Pocket Guide to
Pubs and their History

Pocket Guide to
Pubs and their History

Gordon Thorburn

First published in Great Britain in 2010 by
Remember When
An imprint of
Pen & Sword Books Ltd
47 Church Street
Barnsley
South Yorkshire
S70 2AS

ISBN 978 1 84468 093 1

A CIP catalogue record for this book is
available from the British Library.

Typeset in 10pt Palatino by Mac Style, Beverley, East Yorkshire
Printed and bound in the UK by CPI

Pen & Sword Books Ltd incorporates the imprints of Pen & Sword Aviation,
Pen & Sword Maritime, Pen & Sword Military, Wharncliffe Local History,
Pen & Sword Select, Pen & Sword Military Classics, Leo Cooper, Seaforth
Publishing and Frontline Publishing.

For a complete list of Pen & Sword titles please contact
PEN & SWORD BOOKS LIMITED
47 Church Street, Barnsley, South Yorkshire, S70 2AS, England
E-mail: enquiries@pen-and-sword.co.uk
Website: www.pen-and-sword.co.uk

Contents

Acknowledgements

Many, many thanks for photographs to Peter Bensimon, Margaret Brace, Eric Fleming, Maggie Grey, Mike Greenwood, James Hannen, Marion Nicholson, Frances Thorburn, Andrew Todd, Peter Walkley, Mike Wilde, David Woolley. Special thanks also for wise words from the three Johns – Bjornson, Mann and Murphy.

Preface

'A pub may be calm or boisterous, smart or scruffy, genteel or rough, quiet or noisy, urban or rural, big or small, crowded or empty. No two of the nearly 70,000* in England and Wales are the same. The worst are detestable, the best are unique contributions to human happiness, and among the greatest of British inventions.'

Richard Boston, Beer and Skittles

The first time I went in a pub, I was with my dad and two other blokes. It was sometime in the 1957-58 football season, which would make me 11 or 12 years old, and we were driving back to Scarborough from watching Middlesbrough beat Doncaster Rovers five nil, with a certain B Clough scoring four of them. We stopped off at The Little Angel in Whitby. It's in Flowergate, at the top of Brunswick Street, and I was allowed in because my father until very recently had been a police sergeant in Whitby.

I wasn't allowed beer of course; my first taste of that was a year or two away, and the appropriate drink was deemed to be Kia Ora orange squash. These were Spartan days, when J_2O hadn't been invented and nobody in Yorkshire had heard of Coca-Cola. The soft drinks I knew were dandelion and burdock, cream soda, lemonade and Tizer the Appetiser. Fruit juice was something

---

Plus ça change

… plus c'est la même chose. As the late Richard Boston noted in his estimable work, *Beer and Skittles*: 'Graffiti discovered by archaeologists in Ur of the Chaldees show that the inhabitants thought that the quality of the drink (beer) had deteriorated, and the first legal code ever devised, that of King Hammurabi of Babylon in about 1,750 BC, condemned weak and over-priced ale.'

---

* In 1976. By 2010, down to about 55,000.

adults had as a first course in a restaurant. I would have preferred any of those to orange squash, but I was not consulted.

The men had two or three pints – of what I don't know – while I sat with my orange which, as a favour to my father, had been mixed very strong. By the time it had been topped up and topped up, it was almost entirely Kia Ora with hardly any water.

We were about five miles out of Whitby on the North Yorks Moors when I told my dad I thought I was going to be sick. I was immediately proved right so my words had been, in more than one sense, a Scarborough warning. Doubtless there are many folk who can recall being sick after a visit to the pub early in their drinking careers, but how many can claim to have thrown up on Kia Ora?

My first beer was a taste of a bottle my father was drinking, at about age fourteen. By the time I was seventeen I was, like most of my friends at Scarborough High School for Boys, regularly passing myself off as eighteen and drinking pints of bitter in pubs. I had £1 a week pocket money, which would have bought twelve pints although it never did, two or three on a Friday being considered quite daring enough. After all, I had to drive home on my Vespa 150 and appear sober to my mother.

This latter was quite important to bear in mind, as I'd already alerted her warning systems. I'd been playing cricket for Seamer, an evening game, possibly a cup game, away at Bempton on Flamborough Head. I was sixteen and not very good at cricket, but I was available and my girlfriend was the scorer. Returning from what may have been a victory, the team stopped at a brilliant old roadhouse called The Boak End (pronounced Bork).

This pub, famous and much admired by all in those days, is now an island in a sea of caravan sites and renamed The Dotterel Inn by one of the chains. It was advertised recently for sale: 'The outlet is situated on a major crossroads on the main road between Scarborugh (sic) and Bridlington and the operators need to be able to combine marketing flair to initially attract people into the outlet backed up by quality service and food to encourage repeat business. They should also be able to interact with the local community to provide a solid community base for the outlet.'

As Alan Freeman used to say, not 'arf.

Believing The Boak End to be a pub rather than an outlet, and knowing nothing of marketing flair but hoping to interact later with my girlfriend, I was inundated. The team had decided it was time for an ancient cricketing ritual to be performed, a rite of passage, viz, the getting of a junior player into an advanced emotional state and leaving him on his doorstep for his parents to find. Between them, they bought me six pint bottles of Cameron's Strongarm, which would be enough for most experienced drinkers and more than enough for a callow sixteen-year-old. Deposited on the doorstep as aforesaid, I found myself unable to explain my condition to my mother. I don't think I made it to the great white telephone. Cups of tea and towels cloud my memory.

Of course, getting drunk to vomiting point was never the reason for going into pubs, although nowadays it seems to be like that in cities at weekends. We went under age in pubs because it was a grown-up thing to do and because we liked beer. The beer we had in Scarborough was Cameron's of West Hartlepool, Rose's of Malton and Moors' and Robson's of Hull, known as Muck and Rubbish.

The Scarborough and Whitby Brewery, maker of the famous Target Ales, itself the result of amalgamations and deals among several older firms, including the Esk in Whitby, St Thomas's, the Old Brewery and the Scarborough Brewery Co, had been taken over by Cameron's. The other main Scarborough pub estate, belonging to the Castle and Phoenix Brewery also called Nesfield's, had been swallowed up by Moors' and Robson's in 1932.

There was one Tetley pub which we didn't use much because Tetley's beer 'didn't travel well', and one Bass house I remember, The Aberdeen, closed the last time I looked. All the pubs sold the product now called 'real ale' but nobody called it that because all ale was real. There was no keg beer in the ordinary pubs in Scarborough in 1963 and no draught lager. Lager came in bottles and some girls drank it with lime as a change from Babycham or Cherry B. Very few girls drank beer. My girlfriend's cousin drank pints of Guinness, which caused more amazement than if she had had four legs and a tail.

Regarding ale, real or unreal, I don't think we were very quality minded in any case. We were just glad to be served and to be in a pub. We couldn't get beer anywhere else. There were no supermarkets so no cheap six-packs. Off-licences had bottled beer but would never sell it to anyone obviously under eighteen, and the thought of hanging around the bandstand or whatever, getting drunk, never occurred, mainly because it wasn't possible.

In central Scarborough town now, and on the sea front, 'real ale' is sold in the minority of pubs. Most have only lager and smooth. The Alma, hidden away up a narrow lane just off the corner of Northway and Castle Road, has several good beers and is a proper pub; The New Inn in Falsgrave likewise, even if it's now called The Tap and Spile. The Angel on North Street is OK if you like Tetley's and big screen TV. And so, and so, and the grumpy old pub man regrets the changes in pubs that others seem to welcome.

We lived briefly in North Walsham, Norfolk, an old market town with an old-fashioned look to it. It has five pubs in the centre, and there is not a square inch of any of them, except in the toilets, where you cannot hear piped music, mostly of the boy-racer variety. The biggest pub has music piped into the gents, in case you miss a beat while having a pee.

I could have wept when we moved to where we are now, with our ancient pub that has no music, no machines, no pool table, no anything it didn't have in 1950, 1850 or 1750 for that matter, except an electronic till. The village alone probably wouldn't be enough to keep it open but people come from all over the country to see it and be in it and have a drink in it, because it is what it is, with settles, thatched roof, open fire, beer straight from the barrel. It's a treasure, but why is it a rarity? Why have we had giant screen TVs, loud youf music and smooth foisted on us, when we will travel many miles to find a pub that doesn't have these things?

I was moaning about the music in a North Walsham pub when the seventeen-year-old granddaughter of a friend said, 'If you don't like music, why do you go in pubs?' Which kind of sums it up, really.

When is a pub not a pub?

'When is a drinking place not a pub? The answer to the customer is pretty clear. It is that in any bar where social drinking takes second place, the full requirement is not met. That is to say, not that other activities are always out of place, but rather that if they are allowed to predominate the result will be something less, or at any rate something other, than a pub.'

The Traditional English Pub, Ben Davis

The truth of this judgement is demonstrated by an incident that took place in a central London pub around 1972. The landlord was a large, genial chap, never morose, always forthright, and his pub was very popular. His draught Bass was truly excellent and he did a good lunchtime trade in the chop and mash, pie and peas kind of food, but he had a natural understanding of Ben Davis' principle of predominance. The rule at lunchtime, rigorously applied, was that you ordered your drinks first, then you could go to the large serving hatch and order your meal.

One day, some way, nobody could ever imagine how, a young woman, a stranger, managed to seat herself with her plate of food without having bought a drink. The landlord was on the case straight away. He came out from behind the bar and, with due allowance for her youth and unfamiliarity with house rules, asked her what she'd like to drink.

'Oh' she said. 'Perhaps a glass of water, please.'

'What do you want?' said the landlord. 'A f***ing wash or something?'

CHAPTER ONE

How Did It Happen?

I say, old girl, tea's awfully nice and so on, but how about a pint down the pub?

Three different types of establishment feature in the early history of the pub, and none of them were called pub. In the beginning was the alehouse, followed by the inn and the tavern.

Tavern is from the Latin word *taberna*, by which the Romans generally meant a roadside wine bar with overnight facilities – a kind of inn, in fact. Our tavern was not an inn but rather the saloon bar of the Thirteenth Century. Most towns had several by that time. They sold wine, mainly or exclusively, and charged well for it. The middle and upper-middle strata of the drinking and chattering classes were willing to pay extra, for comfortable surroundings and for not having to rub shoulders with ale-swilling hoi polloi.

The inn, appearing in numbers around the same time although there were earlier examples, was usually an upmarket alehouse with rooms and board. Indeed, there was an obligation on the innkeeper to provide shelter and security to any and all bona fide travellers, and those with the ability and need to travel were, mostly, not of the lower orders.

The word inn changed its meaning as these wayside facilities became more common, from its Anglo-Saxon – inn as a noun just meant dwelling house; as a verb, to lodge – to its modern implication as a place where temporary accommodation and some hearty scoff could be had. The facilities themselves

In Beckley, a picture-postcard village near Oxford, is the **Abingdon Arms**, here shown in 1925 with three Oxford undergrads enjoying the ale and 'the best views in Oxfordshire'. Rather more recent reports credit the pub with keeping to its village traditions although, as with so many, fine food has become much more important to survival.

There is another Abingdon Arms at Wantage, and another at Thame, also Oxfordshire. The Abingdons whose arms they bear are the Earls of that ilk, family name Bertie, title now held by the Earls of Lindsey whose arms appear not to grace any pubs. Hall's Noted Ales have been replaced in Beckley by Brakspear.

Pub Rubbish Korner

Ye, as in Ye Olde Pigges Hedde, is not a word and never was. The only 'ye' to exist in English is an archaic way of saying 'you', the second person pronoun, the plural of 'thou', as in *O come, all ye faithful*. Somewhere along the line, somebody got in a muddle, thus.

The Anglo-Saxons had two single letters to express the 'th' sound. One, called eth, pronounced as in weather, looked like a lower case 'd' with a cross over its upper stem, like this: ð or, as a capital, like this: Ð. The other, called thorn, looked like this þ in both upper and lower case. You might imagine that Anglo-Saxon scribes would use thorn for the thorn sound and eth for the the sound, but the symbols seem to have been interchangeable.

For example, the Anglo-Saxon Chronicle tells us that the elder brother of Alfred the Great was engaging the Danes in 871: 'Ond þæs ymb ii monaþ gefeaht Æþered cyning ond Ælfred his broður wiþ þone here æt Basengum'.

And afterwards, about the second month, King Ethelred and his brother Alfred fought with those raiders at Basing (Hampshire) – and, incidentally, lost.

One sentence later, also in the second month, Alfred *his broður* had become *his broþur*, and he and Ethelred were battling at 'Meretune' (Merton in Surrey), where they were felled and had to flee, regardless of thorn or eth.

Both letters are still used in modern Icelandic but in English eth gradually fell out of favour, displaced eventually and entirely by thorn.

Scribes, wishing to save space on extremely expensive vellum and paper, abbreviated some of the most common words, and 'the' became a thorn with a very small 'e' directly above it. Over the years, thorn opened up and became more and more like a letter 'y', and so you had 'the' represented something like this: y^e, and when printing came in, the same shorthand was a convenient way of saving time and money while making and hand-setting type.

Later, some idiot saw this, and the reste is ye olde hystorie.

also changed, from a large-ish but otherwise ordinary house with very basic sleeping arrangements, to a purpose-designed building, or redesigned/extended alehouse, with stables, bedrooms, dining rooms, meeting rooms and so on.

When is a pub not a pub?

If a pub is a place where social drinking occurs, then the two most intrusive influences on this true purpose are the provision of entertainment, and the provision of food.

Some traditionalist landlords, and customers, would say that any entertainment, beyond that provided naturally by the customers, is an admission of failure, but even they will help organise and/or play in the darts and pétanque teams. Entertainment might be there to help engender atmosphere, as was the case years ago in a pub south of Cambridge where a couple of the bars had loudspeakers, on fairly low, playing classical music. Radio Three in a pub? Well, it worked.

More usually, entertainment is to take extra money from the customers who are already there, as with quiz machines, pool tables etc, or it is to bring in more customers, as with karaoke nights, strippers on Sunday lunchtime, live bands on Saturday nights and so on. In some cases, as might be the case with live bands, the entertainment is a kind of loss-leader. The extra turnover may not match the band's fees but the performance may create regulars.

If landlords pay the enormous fees required for satellite TV and therefore live sport, they may feel they have to have the screens on all the time to get their money's worth, even if the sport is of no interest to anyone in the pub at the time.

As to food – no social drinker wants to sit next to people eating. Also, no drinker likes to wait to be served while some idiot tries to decide between the beef curry and the pie of the day. Also, no drinker likes to see all the tables already laid up for eating. Where do we sit, if we're only having a pint?

The first purpose-made inns were being built by the end of the 1300s and some still survive, such as The George Inn, Norton St Philip, between Bath and Frome. This is not anywhere you would consider building today's equivalent, the economy-price travel lodge, but in those days there seems to have been a lot more going on around Norton St Philip, with fairs, pilgrimages, monasteries and whatnot. The New Inn in Gloucester is another original, from around 1450.

The Fighting Cocks in St Albans is one of several to claim to be the oldest inn in England and it did develop from an early alehouse to an inn, going through several names in the process including The Round House and The Fisherman, and several premises. The Royal Standard of England, near Beaconsfield, claims roots in a Saxon alehouse belonging to the Godwine family, which as every schoolchild used to know, produced the King Harold who lost at Hastings in 1066. Later, the house was much used by drovers and had a communal room for their sleeping but it wasn't until the mid Seventeenth Century that this inn could offer private rooms to guests, and the building you see now, although very old, has had nothing to do with the Godwines or any other Saxons.

The Eagle and Child, Stow-on-the-Wold, claims to have been an inn in the 1200s and before that a hospital and, given Stow's position where main roads met and fairs were held since 1330, it would be surprising if there were no very old inns there, but official records note the first inn in Stow to be The Swan in Sheep Street, open before 1446, closed a long time ago.

Another 'oldest inn' is The Trip to Jerusalem, Nottingham, which isn't an inn at all and certainly isn't as old as claimed, probably by 500 years. Most remarkable of all if it were true, The Bingley Arms in Bardsey, off the Leeds-Wetherby road, claims to have morphed from Saxon alehouse to inn; that is The Priest's Inn, before 1,000 AD.

Oldest or not, there was no such thing as a hotel and the inn industry could only grow as roads improved, civil order became more reliable and more people travelled. Some quite small communities, unimportant apart from being ideal spots for overnight stops on the main roads, became hospitality towns with numbers of inns far beyond anything the residents and near neighbours might require. If you travelled on the Great North Road, you were bound to go through Biggleswade, for example. In 1700, Biggleswade had inns called White Horse, Cross Keys, Bell, White Hart, Crown, King's Arms, Red Lion, Royal Oak, Wrestlers' Arms, Sun and Swan, for a town of less than 1,000 people. Boroughbridge, at a road and river junction, had 22 inns at one time, with The Crown offering stabling for 100 horses while others aimed a little more downmarket at the drovers accompanying Scottish cattle, perhaps 2,000 of the beasts crossing the bridge in a single day.

That there were alehouses in the Ninth and Tenth Centuries cannot be disputed. Laws were passed in connection with them. It must also be the case that some of these very old alehouses were the antecedents of current inns. What cannot be substantiated is that any inn, or pub, now open in Britain stands on the site of any Saxon alehouse, or that any part of its building was once part of the Saxon version.

Alehouses, as the name rather implies, were drinking holes selling ale, which was a simple brew made from malted barley, water and yeast, sometimes with herbs added to help it clarify and keep but not yet with hops. Hops made beer, not ale, and they didn't arrive in any quantity from the Continent until the

The Englishman strays at his peril into the land of eighty shilling heavy, and more so when confronted by a James Adam townhouse, c1794, in Glasgow, with a sign proclaiming it to be **The Babbity Bowster**.

For those readers not familiar with Scottish courting practice in the pre-text message age, the babbity bowster was a dance sometimes performed by the would-be MacRomeo for his intended MacJuliet. More often, it was just one hell of a whirligig played as the finale to a braw nicht at the ball or the wedding.

The name is a shortening of 'Bab at the Bowster', bab being a Scots term of endearment, the equivalent of the Nottingham 'mi duck' or the West Country 'moi loverrr'. Bowster is a Scots pronunciation of bolster, as in pillow. The dance involves ritual words: 'Wha' learn'd you to dance, Bab at the Bowster brawly?'. These words are spoken or sung while kneeling on a cushion or pillow at intervals in the dance, and punctuated by kissing a person, preferably one of the opposite sex, who is also kneeling. A toned-down version is used in Scottish school playgrounds.

1400s nor take over thoroughly as the sine qua non of additives until much later, and that after a struggle.

Here is an eccentric physician called Andrew Boorde, writing in 1542 or thereabouts: 'Beer is made of malt, of hops, and water; it is the natural drink of a Dutchman, and now of late days it is much used in England to the detriment of many English people.' It gave you colic and made you fat and inflated, as Doctor Boorde said you could prove simply by looking at your average Dutchman. On the other hand, 'Ale is made of malt and water, and they which do put any other thing to ale than is rehearsed, except yeast, balm or godisgood, doth sophisticate their ale. Ale for the Englishman is the natural drink.'

By balm he probably meant the herb costmary, also called alecost and balsam herb, which gave the ale a spicier touch. Godisgood was another term for yeast, possibly the working yeast taken from one brew to another. This ale was produced by folk who knew how to do it but not why the system worked.

The ale you drank in the early alehouses, and there were plenty of them, was almost certainly brewed on the premises by the person selling it to you, who was, also almost certainly, a female. She presided over the Medieval equivalent of the public bar, the place of resort of the working classes, also the non-working classes and various ne'er-do-wells and undesirables such as cattle dealers, ladies of the night and writers.

Such an alewife was Elinour Rumming of Leatherhead, immortalised by the poet John Skelton around 1508, many years after the Saxons of course but we have no reason to believe that the nature of the alehouse had changed much. Elinour herself was, it seems, no beauty.

> 'Her face all bowsy,
> Comely crinkled,
> Like a roast pig's ear,
> Bristled with hair.'

Her brew was the title of the poem, *The Tunning of Elinour Rumming*, and anyone with an interest in beer will know that a tun is a barrel or brewing vessel. Elinour's ale was famous in Leatherhead. It was strong and foaming ('nappy' or 'noppy') and all manner of folk came to take it.

> 'She breweth nappy ale
> And maketh thereof pot-sale
> To travellers, to tinkers,
> To sweaters, to swinkers,
> And all good ale-drinkers,
> That will nothing spare
> But drink till they stare
> And bring themseleves bare …
> … Come whoso will
> To Elinour on the hill
> With 'Fill the cup, fill!'
> And sit there by still,
> Early and late.'

They came with bare legs and feet, 'Hardely full unsweet', and unlaced and unbraced, in titters and tatters, some with money, some with their few worldly goods to exchange for nappy ale. To swink, by the way, is to labour and toil, but also to drink copiously. Once again the Remember When imprint does its bit for Scrabble players.

Compared to most earlier brewers or, correctly, brewsters, they being the female of the species, Elinour Rumming was quite a professional. Many alehouses were small, part-time affairs, the availability of a new brew being announced by hanging a bushy arrangement of leaves and twigs on a pole, or ale stake. This ad hoc arrangement for drinking was nothing like the hardship that might be suffered nowadays if the local pub had no beer. There were dozens of these places, country towns and villages were small, and so there were bound to be a few you could find and go to at any given time. In the big cities, like London, Norwich and Exeter, things were better organised and the new trade of tippler was emerging, one who bought ale wholesale from regular brewers and sold it on at a profit.

People used to drink ale or small beer, weak admittedly but brewed nonetheless, at breakfast, dinner and supper, because the boiling of brewing made the water drinkable. Brewing was a routine job done by wives and servants in every household able to do it, and so it is an interesting wonderment that there could be so many pubs at that time. When the 1500s turned into the 1600s, there was a licensed drinking establishment for every 200 or so people, and presumably a goodly number of unlicensed ones. Today, if you include hotel bars and nightclubs, there's a pub for every 1,000 or so. How did that happen?

It's been an up and down story. The first big downer was James I and VI, who came from Scotland to the English throne in 1603 and brought with him the forerunner of that state of affairs we used to have in more recent Scotland, where the only drink to be had on a Sunday was in a hotel bar if you were off your own parish and therefore a traveller. The thing about King James was, he made it every day. Inns, alehouses and taverns were, he decreed, all for the purpose of refreshing those going from A to B, and not for the locals to waste time in, getting puddled when they should be working or praying. Your

> Whoe'er has travell'd life's dull round,
> Where'er his stages may have been,
> May sigh to think he still has found
> The warmest welcome at an inn.
>
> *Written on a Window of an Inn at Henley,*
> William Shenstone, 1714–1763.
> (Possibly The Red Lion, possibly The Angel. Ed.)

> ### He gave her gin just to make her sin
>
> Many years before the village squire had his evil way with poor little Angeline, the juniper berry had been used, at the very beginnings of spirit distillation, to disguise the unpleasant taste of the raw liquors that the early makers produced. Spirits were for medicinal use then, and many centuries passed before the idea caught hold of drinking them for pleasure.
>
> London dry gin is the result of re-distillation to get rid of the flavours of the original materials, which are maize, malted barley and rye, the purer distillate being flavoured with a complex formula, the chief ingredients of which are juniper and coriander.
>
> Dutch gin retains some of the grainy flavours and so is considered less refined by London dry aficionados.

average riff-raff could therefore only drink in these places for one set hour a day. We cannot tell how thoroughly such restrictions were applied in real life but they were not lifted in law until Charles II brought us back to our senses.

Meanwhile, to help pay for the Civil War, the Long Parliament imposed duty on, among other things, beer. This was a tax that had a swingeing effect on small brewers and alehouses that brewed, because they had to stump up the cash in advance. The effect was to reduce the numbers of licensed premises. Meanwhile again, the chaos across the land caused by the war meant that unlicensed premises sprung up.

By 1651, with Charles II up an oak tree and defeated for the moment, and peace and order restored, the licensing authorities got their Acts together and, once again, the numbers dropped of places selling alcohol.

The next major change of course for the good ship pub was all down to gin and the army. Alehouse and innkeepers were obliged by law to billet soldiers and, needless to say, they didn't like it. The money was poor and the soldiers were trouble. As the Duke of Wellington said they were the scum of the earth and, as he may have said, 'I don't know what effect these men will have on the enemy, but by God they frighten me.' Such were the boarders imposed on the pubs of the day, when there were no barracks to put them in.

If that wasn't bad enough, there was a serious threat from unforeseen competition. With our new Dutch King, William of Orange, came a surge in popularity of the juniper-flavoured grain spirit we call gin, formerly known as genever which is more or less the Dutch word for juniper, or Hollands. After

In Warminster, not far from Stonehenge but nearer to an army base, **The Bath Arms** maintains its roots in Seventeenth Century coaching while providing beer and entertainment for the Twenty-first Century soldier. Locals and officers apparently tend to use the lounge bar while other ranks go in the public. Whither the cycling soldier in the 1950 photo, we cannot tell.

Also from 1950: 'Warminster, a pleasant town on the (Wiltshire) borders of Somerset, with a 14th century church, an ancient inn and a 17th century grammar school, lies 400 feet above sea level and is one of the most bracing inland resorts in the south-west of England. There is excellent hunting in the neighbourhood, and a golf course 700 feet above sea level.' *British Railways Holiday Guide*

There are three Bath Arms in the district, with the Marquess thereof being close by at Longleat, plus others at Frome, Cheddar, Shrewsbury and Brighton.

an Act of 1690, anybody could distil and sell gin if it was from English grain, and that was the year they doubled the duty on beer.

Feeble efforts were made to control the gin trade but it all went crackers. 'Drunk for a penny, dead drunk for tuppence' was the cry.

A brief diversion upon the subject of government duty on alcohol

The proportion of alcohol in beverages naturally affects their drinking properties but also offers governments a convenient measure by which to levy duty.

Such a possibility first occurred to the British government in the late 1600s, as a better and fairer way than simply taxing beer in general, but if the idea was to be turned into revenue, some sort of measurable standard was needed. It was too difficult then to make perfectly pure alcohol (ethanol) as a reference point, a benchmark as it were; it would always be slightly dilute. So, it was decided that a half-and-half mixture of (notionally) pure alcohol and rainwater would be the standard, and the integrity of this benchmark spirit would be proved, not by swigging, but by pouring some onto a small heap of gunpowder. If it was impossible to light the wet powder, the spirit was too watery. If it burned nice and steadily with a blue flame, that was proof that the spirit was as it should be. If the spirit was a little too strong there would be a crackle and a pop and yellow flames. If it was much too strong, hats and facial hair would be lost.

It is not known how this quite brilliant standard test came about. Did they fiddle around with proportions of alcohol and rainwater until the mixture would allow gunpowder to burn, and lo, it turned out to be exactly 50:50? Or did one fellow in the office happen to know that a 50:50 mixture would just allow ignition in the blend of powder he used in his hunting musket? Or, more likely, does it go back to around 1420 and the process of corning gunpowder?

A problem with gunpowder before that time lay with its very powderiness. Unless handled by a highly skilled gunner, it often would not discharge properly, or at all. It needed air in the mix, and the answer was to make it into granules, or 'corn'. The powder was moistened, packed and shaped into a cake, and forced through a sieve with different sized holes according to the powder's destination – fine for pistols, say, or coarse for ships' cannon. The best gunpowder moisteners were adjudged to be wine or other alcoholic drink, and urine. Best of all was wine drinker's urine. Here must surely be hidden the science which led to the definition of proof spirit.

While the definition remained and remains the same, the British authorities eventually developed an easier and more accurate method of proving it, presumably after the wives of scorched Excise men complained that a kiss without a moustache was like a ham sandwich without mustard. A gallon of the proof spirit that burned with gunpowder was found to weigh 7lb 12oz at 51° Fahrenheit. This measure was a little on the cumbersome side too, so a use was at last found for an instrument that had been awaiting a serious purpose since Archimedes leapt from his bath around 220 BC.

In 1675, Robert Boyle (he of the Law) had translated Archimedes' Principle, that the apparent loss of weight of a body immersed in a fluid is equal to the

The Bear Inn, Faversham, photographed here in 1901 complete with ghostly dog, is still largely seen as 'unspoiled' and 'a proper pub' by most reports, and is still serving Shepherd Neame as you would expect the brewery having been in the town since 1698.

Signs of the Bear generally could be connected to the arms of the local bigwig, in which case there might often be a colour – Black Bear – or an heraldic addition – Bear and Ragged Staff. A market place position like this and the simplest version of the name would suggest a link to the old Sunday morning pursuit of bear-baiting, made illegal in 1835 but much enjoyed in earlier times. Queen Elizabeth I was a particular fan of this game, as they called it then.

There are about 65 pubs that are plain Bear, plus another 100 or so that are sorts of Bears – White, Brown and so on – or that have an addition – Bear and Staff, Dog and Bear, the latter obviously also linked to bear-baiting. It should be pointed out that fighting cocks and dogs, baiting bears and bulls and like games were made illegal, not through any concerns for the welfare of the animals, but in an attempt to curb the betting and the coarse and rowdy behaviour of the spectators.

weight of the fluid displaced, into his new and improved hydrometer. Properly graduated for the job, it would be able to measure how much alcohol there was in the gin, or how much solid matter there was in the milk or, if it came to it, how dirty was the bath water.

The hydrometers of the period indeed were reliable in telling if a spirit was bob-on proof or not, but they were not accurate enough to measure by how much a spirit might be over or under. Their design also assumed that the spirit being measured consisted solely of alcohol and water; they could not take account of non-watery ingredients. Dastardly merchants added 'weight' to their spirits with, say, molasses, to lower the apparent amount of alcohol they'd have to pay duty on.

Since all drinking spirits were well under proof and contained material other than water, such hydrometers were not the ideal tax-gatherer's aid. A plea went forth in 1802 for an accurate hydrometer which would be easy to use with the whiskies, brandies, gins and rums of the time, with simply interpreted results. Bartholemew Sikes won the competition; his hydrometer was officially adopted by an Act of 1816 and it is still in use today.

Now that it could the Act also re-described the standard, the proof spirit, as one which at 51°F weighed twelve thirteenths of the same amount of distilled water. The men drafting the Act forgot to specify the temperature of the water but that was presumed to be 51°F also.

Subsequent analysis showed that proof spirit was not exactly 50:50 alcohol:water, but 49.28:50.72 by weight at 60°F. Metrically minded folk might have equalised the definition but instead a different way was found of looking at the one they had. Studies showed that 100 volumes of pure alcohol diluted to proof strength at 50°F resulted in 175.36 volumes, which set up the system of degrees for giving the strengths of various alcoholic drinks, not of 180° as often thought but 175°. Older readers will remember when normal Scotch, gin and so on was labelled as being 70° proof, that is 70 parts by volume out of 175, or precisely 40% ABV as the label says nowadays.

In the United States, proof spirit is 50:50 alcohol and water by volume, and that logic is extended into a labelling system based on two hundreds. A whisky given as 40% ABV in the European system has traditionally been called 80-proof in the USA but our percentage by volume, or Gay-Lussac, system is gradually being adopted there.

Those who would be served whisky at 70° proof in quantities of one sixth of a gill (one fifth in Scotland) and multiples thereof, in tribute to Fifteenth Century gunpowder manufacturers, rather than whisky at 40% ABV and 25 millilitres, are nothing more than incurably romantic old fools.

Back to the history of pubs

The alehouse owners responded to the competitive threat of gin in the only way they knew how: they started selling it too. Tobias Smollet, a novelist and surgeon from Dumbarton, completed his *History of England* in three volumes in 1758 and had this to say about the London suburbs, areas we should now regard as central London: '(they) abounded with an incredible number of public houses, which continually resounded with the news of riot and intemperance. They were the haunts of idleness, fraud and rapine, and the seminaries of drunkenness, debauchery, extravagance, and every vice incident to human nature.'

At about the same time, Dr Samuel Johnson was saying, 'There is nothing which has yet been contrived by man, by which so much happiness is produced as by a good tavern or inn', and Oliver Goldsmith was writing *The Deserted Village*:

> 'Near yonder thorn, that lifts its head on high,
> Where once the signpost caught the passing eye,
> Low lies that house where nut-brown draughts inspired,
> Where grey-beard mirth, and smiling toil retired,
> Where village statesmen talked with looks profound,
> And news much older than the ale went round.
> Imagination fondly stoops to trace
> The parlour splendours of that festive place:
> The white-washed wall, the nicely sanded floor,
> The varnished clock that clicked behind the door.'

The latter two luminaries were writing about a kind of hostelry that was easily distinguished from buildings around it in country or town: the inn or tavern. Indeed, Johnson's chronicler Boswell was quite adept at distinguishing which might offer the best in entertainment, at one point ignoring The Lamb and Flag in Covent Garden and heading instead for a tavern called The Shakespeare's Head, now gone but then providing Boswell with two professional girls for the price of a bottle of sherry. Covent Garden was a hot spot for such activities, where a wine licence might allow a taverner with entrepreneurial spirit to broaden the scope of attractions in the same way as one might now install satellite television.

Smollet was railing against the worst of the common alehouses that came and went with the fortunes of the proprietor, who may himself have been every bit as idle, intemperate and extravagant as his customers, but as we reached the final years of the Eighteenth Century, things began to change in London and the other big cities. The larger brewers saw that size mattered and various deals

Signs of Old Times: The SUV and Half

This ancient wayside inn is handy for the farmers round about but they prefer to go the extra two miles into town to The Mended Bucket. The local fuzz apply the breathalyser enthusiastically so people from town don't come here either. Plenty of space is thus assured for holidaymakers and their children from the caravan site, who like to keep within view of the big-screen satellite TV while playing with their Playstations and spreading their Lego across the huge single bar-room that used to be public, saloon, snug and smoke room.

On Sunday lunchtimes, one end of the bar is reserved for the local government officials, journalists and call-centre managers from the neo-Georgian flag-poled estate where Low Rutter Farm used to be. They discuss motorcars and personal computers, with lawn mowers and pond linings occasionally allowed as guest subjects.

At The SUV and Half, food is served strictly 12 noon-2pm and 6pm-9pm. The menu offers panoply of international exotica. Moussaka, curry, chilli con carne, sweet and sour pork and shepherd's pie are all served with a Ping! in little oval dishes. To accompany, you can have chips, rice or jacket, and the small heap of salad with a slice of orange cooks rapidly on the searingly hot plates, so eat that first.

The attractive female bar staff will leave their private conversations and text messaging if asked, to serve from a selection of seven different lagers, an Irish keg bitter and numerous varieties of brightly coloured liquids allegedly flavoured with lychees, pawpaws, starfruit and so on. On a cork notice board are colour postcards also showing attractive females but nude and kneeling in the sea.

The landlord, originally a car salesman from Basildon, spends a great deal of money at the hairdresser's and affects a nice line in gold necklaces, medallions and bangles. As you can easily observe, he has a hairy chest. He normally wears white leather slip-on shoes but also has a fawn pair. Soon he will sell his pub to the owner of the caravan site and his like will never be seen again.

were done which produced fewer but bigger and stronger brewery companies. With their size came an increased requirement to assure their sales; they rescued profligate landlords with cheap mortgages and increased security, or provided low-cost loans for refurbishment, all under contract obliging the

Bad pub guides

Every so often, the quality national papers produce supplements purporting to guide us to marvellous pubs. These supplements have several interesting things in common:

1. You never see the same pub recommended by more than one newspaper.
2. Despite being well travelled in the UK and a regular pub goer, you have never been to any of the pubs mentioned.
3. The write-ups are clearly done by someone who has never been to them either.

For example, The Royal Oak in Ripon, central North Yorks, cathedral capital of Wensleydale, as far from the coast as it is possible to be in that part of the world, was described by *The Daily Telegraph* as having a menu featuring local produce such as chorizo and sea bream. *The Guardian* suggested wrapping up warm should you want to visit a pub in Diss, south Norfolk, because the sea breezes could give you a chill. Diss is about 25 miles as the breeze blows from the nearest seaside.

Similarly, in one of these supplements, The Fleece Inn, Haworth, was wrapped by the Yorkshire moors when it's actually in the Pennines, and the Yorkshire Dales were 'a pleasant hike away'. Well, Airedale is, but if you want Swaledale and Wensleydale you'd better pack a tent and some provisions for your hike and take a few days off work.

Actually, Rule Two isn't true. Of *The Guardian*'s 100 'Summer Country' pubs, this writer had been to The Old Nag's Head in Edale, The Tan Hill, the Brancaster White Horse, and The Lord Nelson in Burnham Thorpe, or Burham as they had it. Likewise of *The Daily Telegraph*'s '70 Great British Pubs', The Black Friar in EC4 was known, also The George SE1, The Lord Nelson, Burnham Thorpe (dammit, that's Rule One gone as well), The Speedwell in Dundee, and The Duke of York in Whitby. Rule Three, however, remains secure.

landlord to buy his beer from one source only. The tied-house system had started.

Such schemes did not produce the desired effect quickly enough and, from the early years of the Nineteenth Century, a new phenomenon appeared with increasing frequency: the purpose-built public house, a term by now universal

The sign for **The Board Inn**, Whaley Bridge, is devoted to pub games, not all of them played on boards. The man depicted, a master of ceremonies or lord of misrule, wears a billiard-marker as a hat and carries an ivory tusk, raw material for billiard balls and chess pieces. The board for chess is there, and one for backgammon, and a stylised dartboard, but he has also brought his artist's kit with him, his palette and brushes and, it seems, he leans elegantly on a case containing his easel.

among the common herd if not in literature and parliament. Gin shops led the way, with gas lighting, luxurious interiors and, novelty indeed, the bar-counter. A new efficiency swept the trade. Instead of a pot man peering through the candle-lit, smoke-filled gloom to see if anyone wanted him to fetch some beer from the cellar, customers went up to a gas-lit bar and ordered beer to be pulled from a handpump, the recently invented beer engine.

In the old alehouse, there had been no distinction between private and public rooms; you drank your ale in the proprietor's kitchen or parlour. The move to separate rooms by category was already well underway by 1800 and the new pubs confirmed and elaborated it, with their club rooms, smoke rooms, games rooms and so on and, good heavens above, urinals. A revolutionary idea, that pubs should be fit for their purpose, was taking a strong hold.

The Duke of Wellington's Tory government in 1830 took duty off beer and liberalised the licensing laws to such an extent that there was a beer rush, with thousands of new alehouses opening and cheap ale flowing in floods. This was a time of vivid imagination as regards pub names. Most of the common names were well established; the Crowns and the Red Lions and the Royal Oaks and the King's Heads and the Marquis of This and That, and these would not do for new pubs trying to get noticed. Many became Victoria and quite a few became Albert; about 250 and 100 respectively still exist, but you'll struggle to find half a dozen named after the both of them even if you include the museum. There are no restrictions on what you can call your pub beyond a few considerations of modesty, legality and, er, good taste, any more than there are on what you

Older readers will remember when you went to the Jug and Bottle, usually a particular side-door of the pub opening onto a tiny room with a hatchway, where you proffered a jug for filling up with beer for home consumption. There are still a couple of pubs called The Jug and Bottle, and more with the legend on a stained glass window.

There are quite a few Bottle and Glasses, Cock and Bottles, Cork and Bottles and Leather Bottles, also Leathern Bottles, but there's only one Three Bottles, one Bottle Inn, and one

The Bottle House, here in Penshurst, Kent. It is said to be named after a rhyme that used to be on the sign:

> From this bottle I am sure
> You'll get a glass both good and pure.
> Each good man and eke his spouse
> Drink to each other and this house.

call your children. In fact pub namers have more freedom than parents. Even those mums and dads who appear to allocate names to offspring by throwing Scrabble tiles in the air, might hesitate to call their child The Case is Altered, The Frog and Nightgown or The Lady of Shalott.

Wellington's Beer Act was meant to stimulate trade but, as ever, the best laid schemes o' mice an' men went wildly agley. Governments spent the next century trying to put the monster back in the box with gradual increases in controls of various sorts on licensing, on the licensees, on drinking hours, duty, minimum standards for premises, and forbidding the sale of alcohol to children except in sealed containers to be consumed off the premises.

The Temperance Movement had its supporters and even those moderates who did not want prohibition may still have felt that things were a little out of hand. As the general pressure was to reduce, or not to allow an increase of, the number of licensed premises the brewers became more anxious to get hold of the ones that were already there. They floated themselves on the Stock

Exchange to raise money to buy pubs. Property prices rose, and collapsed. The concept of need came in; when a license was up for renewal, the justices of the peace asked if the locale really needed this local. If a brewer wanted to build a posh new pub in an area that didn't have one, he might have to give up two of his old licences from areas over-served by pubs.

The new pubs naturally didn't have the years of trade build-up which had seen the older ones become used as courtrooms, markets, political meeting halls, hubs for all sorts of trades, venues for bear-baiting and suchlike, prize fights and theatrical productions, and essential calls for every travelling showman, quack and hustler. As officialdom became more organised and self-important, town halls and courthouses supplanted the old inns as temples of justice, the

Signs of Old Times: The Cumptoneau Arms

At one time the drinking hole of the Marquis of Cumptoneau's estate workers, this 200-year-old, dual-carriageway-side pub now exists entirely on passing trade, mostly journalists and commercial travellers. The eight different real ales are all cloudy and sour due to lack of throughput, which in turn is due to lack of customers, which in turn is due to the landlord being an early-retirement human resources manager who doesn't really like people very much.

The landlady, once a gorgeous blonde PR girl with a cigarette firm, is now an expert on malt whisky, red wine, premium lager and gin and will always be happy to test a sample with anyone who asks her.

The Cumptoneau Arms is the last resting place of the home-made steak and kidney pie, viz. a small, ping-able oval dish filled with dark brown fluid in which lurk a few lumps of bovine gristle. On top of the dish, but not attached to it, is a pale beige, oval object about six inches high and only fractionally heavier than air, which looks like something growing on a fallen trunk in ancient woodland.

The electric, flickering, pretend-candle wall lights cause migraines while illuminating the pair of plastic duelling pistols and the brass coal scuttles filled with pampas grass. Customers operating the free music machine can choose between James Last playing Mozart or the London Symphony Orchestra playing The Beatles.

Soon, the landlord will die from sheer misery and his lady wife will sell to Snuggle Inns, which will build an extension of Spartan bedrooms for those journalists and commercial travellers already mentioned.

railways took the carriage trade, theatres took the players and blood sports were largely outlawed. Numbers of these inns and alehouses decreased but that central role in the community remained and remains, of the place where you can buy and sell anything and always find someone who can do the job you want, for cash.

One almost unnoticed Victorian reform echoes a recent attempt by our government to civilise drinking and make us more relaxed and less excessive, in a continental kind of café culture. The Whig Chancellor of the Exchequer in 1860, a certain William Ewart Gladstone, introduced the Refreshment Houses and Wine Licences Act, which he hoped would increase the sale of wine at the expense of gin and strong beer so that, by means of 'cleaner channels for consumption', a greater proportion of the populace might enjoy the cultivating effects of wine, reaching 'the whole middle classes, of the lowest order of the middle classes, and even of the better portion of the working classes'.

> 'Over the cobbles he clattered and clashed in the dark inn-yard,
> He tapped with his whip on the shutters, but all was locked and barred.
> He whistled a tune to the window, and who should be waiting there
> But the landlord's black-eyed daughter,
> Bess, the landlord's daughter,
> Plaiting a dark red love-knot into her long black hair.'
>
> *The Highwayman*, Alfred Noyes

In 1869, parliament passed the Wine and Beerhouse Act in an attempt to counter the beer house free-for-all created by Wellington's Act and to clean up the pub business generally. All landlords, with or without daughters, were required to obtain a formal licence from the magistrates if they were to sell beer. The bench had four good reasons for refusal:

- the landlord was unable to provide evidence of his good character;
- the pub, or other near-by premises owned or occupied by the landlord, could be described as disorderly and/or frequented by undesirables such as prostitutes and thieves (and highwaymen, presumably);
- the landlord had been refused on another occasion;
- the pub wasn't fit for its purpose under the law (there was a minimum rateable value, for instance).

Something like 6,000 landlords of pubs lost their licences over the next two years for these reasons.

> ### *No Comment in London*
>
> 'Down to a year or two ago, men found it eminently worth while to seek out the Compton Arms, off Canonbury Lane, for the purpose of inspecting a truly wondrous collection of natural curiosities, as also assegais and other relics of the Zulu War that thrust themselves upon one's view in all the bars. To the intense regret of Islingtonians generally these have utterly vanished. Nowadays the sole distinctive feature of the Compton Arms is a huge aeroplane propellor affixed to the frontage, as it seems to us, for no comprehensible reason.'
>
> *More London Inns and Taverns*, Leopold Wagner, 1925
>
> The Compton Arms remains, without propellor (sic) but with a sign proclaiming it 'Islington's only real pub'. Islingtonians generally can here inspect a truly wondrous collection of natural curiosities on Arsenal match days.

Other pressures on the old trade came from new hotels, designed for the job with all modern conveniences; from gentlemen's clubs, where the top end of the market could go without having its pockets picked; and from another newcomer, restaurants, also appealing to the better class of customer. Laws were passed prohibiting the use of public houses for official business, such as inquests and parish council meetings, unless there was absolutely nowhere else. The pub trade responded by going for the lowest common denominator, gin, and for the mass market. Gin shops, each more splendid than the last, were built anew, or converted from older pubs, or added to them. As Charles Dickens observed, the poorer the district in which they were, the flashier and more luxurious the fixtures and fittings.

The one type of fitting these gin palaces lacked was seating arrangements. Such places were not meant for social drinking, for conversation, for greybeard mirth and smiling toil retired. No, these were the equivalent of the loudest, most brassy city-centre bars today, and their purpose from the landlord's point of view was to sell as much booze as possible in the shortest time to as many customers as might be fitted in, hence the customers standing up. From the customers' point of view, the purpose was to get bladdered.

The Britons Protection, a famous Victorian pub in Manchester, largely unaltered from its origins, is often paired with The Peveril of the Peak (q.v.) as one of the two most visited pubs in the region. While other pubs have been refurbished, modernised, knocked into one room and closed, The Britons and its like remain the same, and crowded.

The lighting, the mirrors, the mahogany, the plate glass, the brass, the mosaics, the extravagant bar counters and all the showy innovations of the gin palace soon filtered into the building and refurbishment of normal pubs, and rather became what we think of as the Victorian pub style. Also, as the gin craze ran its course, gin palaces had to sort themselves out a bit or, as a modern business executive might put it, re-determine their stance in the market place in terms of new product solutions. Two of the most splendid survivors in this style might be The Salisbury in Harringay and The Archway Tavern on the old A1, below Highgate. By the beginning of the Twentieth Century the pub as we know it had settled into its identity, and largely without there being special variants devoted to gin or beer.

Now, more than 100 years on, we lament the vandalism inflicted upon pubs by brewers with silly notions about modernising and corporate identity, freehouse landlords with similarly misled reforming zeal, town planners, city fathers and all the other parties who cannot let things be. In this writer's youth in the town of Scarborough, there were two very fine hotels with bars, The Pavilion, with its separate pub vaults, and the Balmoral, where the cricketers often stayed during the festival. The Pavilion, a fine stone building of great quality, was the first thing you saw when coming out of the railway station. Today, in its place, you see a totally characterless, anonymous eyesore of a miserable shopping centre. Where once stood the lovely red-brick Balmoral in the heart of town, and the old Scarborough and Whitby Brewery, there is an equally undistinguished Tesco. This, ladies and gentlemen, is called development. The city fathers of Scarborough who permitted it cannot now be called to account and we can only hope, rather than expect, that a lesson has been learned.

Wiser counsel prevailed in other parts, and we can still go and marvel at The Princess Louise in Holborn, The Philharmonic in Liverpool, The Prospect of Whitby and The Lamb in Lamb's Conduit Street. We can go to Whitelock's, off Briggate in Leeds, and hope that something dreadful will happen to whoever has threatened to turn it into a wine bar for what they termed the 30-something, BMW-owning set. Such an idea is just as brainless as the one that afflicted so many publicans in the 1970s, who believed that if they put down a carpet and fitted parchment lampshades, a whole different crowd of people, an undiscovered tribe as it were, would flock to the new lounge bar and order scampi in a basket and Martini and lemonade.

This is not to say that a pub needs to be Victorian, or 'period' in any other way, to be a good pub. What it does need to be is the kind of place with which you can have a relationship. A lot depends on the people who run it and work in it, and on the way the space is divided up. The beer is important, even for non-beer drinkers, because of the superior conversation you get in a pub with good beer. These days, food is important too in many pubs, even for those who don't eat it, because without it the pub might be forced to close.

To see the crux of the matter, consider the difference between a supermarket and a pub, not in size but in spirit. The supermarket is not, and can never be, more than its basic nature allows. It's a shop. You go in, buy a few things,

---

No Comment in London

Decidedly remodelled at some point, The Hog in the Pound, South Molton Street W1, is the only pub of that name. A butcher had the premises once upon a time and pigs were kept for slaughter in a pound. His sign showed a fat specimen in a sty, and that was kept when it became an inn.

Bloodshed remained in the reputation for many years because a prostitute called Catherine Hayes, also said to be a barmaid at the Hog, with the help of two men got her husband drunk and cut off his head. They threw that in the Thames and the rest of the body in a pond in Marylebone Fields, but the head was found, identified, and Mrs Hayes was found guilty of Petty Treason, as the murder of a husband by a wife was classified in those days. She was burned alive at the stake at Tyburn, May 9, 1726 (bottom of Edgware Road, Marble Arch). The usual favour of strangulation before burning was denied her, the flames bursting out unexpectedly and beating back he who would have administered this mercy.

The Cat and Fiddle on the Macclesfield/Buxton road, at 1,690 feet is the second highest pub in England, after Tan Hill. These days it is a magnet for bikers, who love seeing if they can get round the bends of this wiggly mountain pass at high speed without falling off.

Other distinguished visitors have included the philosopher Bertrand Russell, who came here in 1916 for three days of discussions on the meaning of life with the young and very beautiful Lady Constance Malleson, wife of actor Miles Malleson. Russell at age 44 was more than twice Constance's age, and he was married, although separated, and he was also having a little dalliance with Lady Otteline Morrel and various others. Constance too was anything but constant, better known as the notably promiscuous actress Colette O'Neil.

There are fewer than a dozen Cat and Fiddles although the familiarity of the name might suggest more. Fox and Fiddle, Pig and Fiddle, Fish and Fiddle, Lion and Fiddle – these names also occur in ones and twos, possibly in a whimsical attempt to be different.

Following the principle that there is more rubbish written about the origins of pub names than anything else, we find that this one is connected with the Duke of Devonshire who regularly stopped here, at the highest point on the road home to Chatsworth House in Derbyshire, to play his violin.

There is another rather fanciful idea that it is a contraction of Catherine la Fidele, Catherine the Faithful aka Catherine of Aragon. Or, it might be a reference to the game of tipcat, a very ancient sport indeed, which uses a wooden peg, sharpened at both ends, instead of a ball. This, called the cat, is placed on the ground and tipped, that is struck hard on one end with a stout stick or specially made bat, so that it flies up. The tipper must then whack the cat again in mid-air, trying to hit it as far as possible. The rules thereafter vary, sometimes involving guessing exactly how far the cat has flown, sometimes making the tipper run round bases as in rounders/baseball, or between points as in cricket. If the tipper misses his shot a certain number of times, usually three, he's out. The difficulty here is explaining the fiddle; some say that at tipcat tournaments there would have been music and dancing. Hm, well, possibly.

Without any assistance from eccentric dukes, Spanish princesses or arcane pub sports, alehouses with cat-fiddling names and signs appeared in London and elsewhere by the early 1600s. This was almost certainly through nothing more fantastical than the proprietor of the house knowing a certain rhyme and liking the name, in the same way that an early motor manufacturer would have preferred Armstrong Siddely Sapphire to Armstrong Siddely Limestone.

So, it is the origins of the rhyme that might lead us to the truth, and those origins must be older than the early 1600s although not necessarily by much.

In those days, holding particular opinions could have you in the deepest trouble. Allegorical or coded nonsense was one way of expressing dangerous ideas. It is possible that 'High diddle diddle', as it then was, formed the harmless-seeming intro to a satirical review of Queen Elizabeth I's alleged affair with Robert Dudley, Earl of Leicester, she being the cat making the music and he being the little dog that laughed to see such fun.

Equally, or maybe more than equally, it is possible that the rhyme has no more significance than an owl and a pussycat going to sea in a beautiful pea-green boat, giving rise to four pubs named thereafter, or a girl just a-walking down the street singing doowah diddy diddydum diddydoo, giving rise to no pub names at all.

and come out. You do that in a pub too, but it's the rest of the experience that makes the difference.

Some time ago, The Swan at Homersfield, a tiny village on the Norfolk/ Suffolk border, was run by an ex-copper, as quite a few pubs used to be. Each year, there was a heaviest marrow competition: not the marrow of greatest dimensions, but the heaviest. Each year, the landlord provided a small ceramic marrow on a plinth as the prize, and each year a chap called John McVicar, who lived in the nearby Suffolk village of Saint Cross South Elmham won the prize. The landlord decided that this wouldn't do. He carefully cut off a small piece from the end of his own entry, inserted an iron bar and glued the piece back on. At the weigh-in, the subterfuge was discovered, Mac won again and, do you know, nobody minded a bit.

At one point in life, your correspondent was responsible for organising the bar at the three or four do's held in any given year at the village hall. This was on his own condition that he would have to attend no committee meetings. The then landlord of The Royal Oak, Appleby-in-Westmorland, was Colin Cheyne, who frequently found the said correspondent in his pub but not necessarily many others from that particular village, which had had no pub of its own since The Kangaroo closed in the 1930s. Colin used to get the licence for the village-hall bar from the magistrates and he would supply all the beer, lager, spirits, wines, optics, glasses, towels and so on at, it was assumed, a reasonable profit to himself. Certainly the village hall made a good profit. It was only later that the discovery was made that Colin had supplied the drink at cost and the glasses and all the rest for nothing.

When the cricket team started at The Cherry Tree, Harleston, Norfolk, it was initially difficult to get a team up, then it became more popular and the question of selection arose. Selection? This, as a journalist might have put it, could have become a minefield the size of Wales. The captain, in consultation with nobody, decided that a week before every match he would put up the list of known players, invite anyone else to add his name provided he was not

---

No Comment in London

'A stranger surveying the market throng in Beresford Square (Woolwich) could scarcely fail to be struck by the number of taverns round about. Not a few of these display signs in keeping with the staple industry of the Arsenal Town or the Defence of the Realm, as witness: the Ordnance Arms, the Gun, the Royal Mortar, the Woolwich Infant, the Armstrong Gun, the Barrack, and the Fortune of War. Among the rest the Salutation, the Shakespeare, the Royal Oak, the Bull, the Bricklayers' Arms, the Elephant and Castle, the Pioneer, the Duke of York and the Duchess of Wellington may be mentioned.'

More London Inns and Taverns, Leopold Wagner, 1925

At the time of writing, The Woolwich Infant is still there but closed. There is an Elephant and Castle but it is not the same one, being part of a modern development. The Bull remains, and one of those listed by Mr Wagner, The Ordnance Arms, is now O'Connor's, the only Victorian pub left actually on the square, and that's all, folks.

The daft business of 'Ye Olde' is dealt with elsewhere (see page 13). Modern folk may wonder, should they base their wonderment on the Cheshire cheese available in a supermarket plastic wrapper, why anyone would want to name a pub after it, but things were not ever thus and cheese was not always made in a chemical works where it's double Gloucester today, Stilton tomorrow and Lancashire the day after.

The most famous of the twenty pub Cheshire Cheeses is probably the one in a little alleyway called Wine Office Court, off Fleet Street, into which Dr Johnson used to pop from his residence around the corner. There are a good half dozen more in Cheshire, four in neighbouring Derbyshire, and all the rest seem to be either in other northern counties or in London.

The Cheese pictured is at Castleton, Derbyshire, and is clearly popular with characters from the film *Mary Poppins*. There may have been an alehouse on this site as early as 1577 although the present building, erected in 1660, reverted to a farmstead before being born-again sometime before 1748 when we know it had a full licence as The Waggon and Horses, by which name it was known for a century until it was changed to The Cheshire Cheese. At that time there were five licensed premises in Castleton, the others being The Nag's Head, The Bull's Head, The Butchers' Arms and The George and Dragon. The Nag and the Cheese have both become Ye Olde, but the Bull remains plain.

currently playing cricket regularly for an official team, and add the instruction that the first eleven names ticked would be the team. He ticked his own name of course, and the landlord's. The landlord always played, he being good at golf.

In this same pub, the landlord suddenly designated the lifeboat charity collection as a swear box. It wasn't a pub where there was a lot of swearing but mine host thought he detected a trend of increase. The lady who collected the lifeboat each quarter was used to writing out a thank-you receipt for six or seven quid. In its first quarter as a swear box, the lifeboat, so heavy the lady could hardly lift it, yielded something like £35.

This was an aspect of his decision that the landlord hadn't really thought about. The small, elegant, refined old lady, volunteer for the RNLI almost since its inception and collector of the money box for a century at least, might not have liked the idea of her takings being tainted by rough words. Luckily for him, he didn't have to explain, she being far too well mannered to ask why generosity towards lifeboatmen had increased sevenfold in three months on the Norfolk/Suffolk border, the nearest lifeboat house being at Southwold, twenty miles away

---

Pub Rubbish Korner

True story. The landlady of a certain pub in what used to be Westmorland, had the environmental health inspectors round: three of them. They had come specially to ask her details of something they called her 'total meat supply chain solution'. After several questions, she realised that they wanted to know how she got her fresh meat for the pub, for her steak dinners, sausage toad and so on. She said she employed a fairly direct method, as it was a short, straight supply chain solution. She rang the butcher up, told him what she wanted, and the butcher delivered it in his van.

Aha, said the inspectors. Was the van refrigerated? Yes, it was. It had a big box thing on the roof, which she knew was the refrigeration unit. How did the meat get from the van to the kitchen? Through the back door. No, no, how was it conveyed? It was conveyed on a large, willow pattern, vintage carving plate, kept in the kitchen especially for meat-conveying duties. The butcher came in, took the plate, which was where it always was, went to his van, piled on the meat, and conveyed it back.

Yes, but how was it conveyed exactly, on the large carving plate? Well, sometimes the butcher operated his intergalactic dematerialiser and beamed it down. Sometimes he threw it like a frisbee. More usually, he carried it in his hands, from the van, through the back door, and into the kitchen.

Aha and double aha, said the inspectors. Were the plate, and its meat, and the hands, all totally enclosed in a sterile disposable plastic membrane for the open-air journey from van to pub door?

Readers are invited to guess the landlady's answer.

Formerly the head office of the **Constant Service Water Company**, this alehouse must be prized as an example of Brighton's rare collection of one-off pub names. Of all towns, Brighton offers the easiest and longest pub crawl of unique nomenclature, including The Lion and Lobster, The No Man Is An Island, The Martha Gunn, The London and Brighton Hog, The Fish Bowl – see also Hector's House, The Geese and The Greys below – but it must be said that some are renamed old pubs, transformed to attract the youthful majority of the Brighton population.

At first, the scale of fees payable to the lifeboat had an effect only on the most expensive swearwords. Soon, such extreme vulgarisms were heard hardly at all, but compensatory income was ensured by increased use of cheaper and less offensive words. The lifeboat continued to offer up its quarterly plentiful cargo but, inevitably, the landlord saw another potential embarrassment arising. Swearing in toto was definitely going down. It had come to a quarter of its peak, nay, less than that, possibly even a seventh. How could he explain such a shortfall? Surely even the lifeboat lady would not be able to resist asking why her money had disappeared and gone back to its level of old.

Bring back the wooden mushrooms

'What can one say of the miscellaneous, extraneous, intercutaneous infestation of juke boxes, one-armed bandits, pin tables and amusement machines which now buzz, click, bleep, chatter and caterwaul in almost every bar of the land? Like vermin they multiply, and like parasites they threaten the essential bodily functions on which the health of a pub must depend.'

The Traditional English Pub, Ben Davis

Of course there have always been pub games. If a cartoonist wishes to imply a pub as the situation for his joke, he draws a couple of pump handles and a dartboard. Your correspondent can remember trying, in vain, to play shove ha'penny in a pub in Highgate, on a serious board used in pub leagues which was made of slate and heated, and the pub's ha'pennies were polished to a mirror finish. Our crude and brutish efforts were no use with such sophisticated equipment. The ha'pennies were out of our control.

The Rising Sun, King's Cross, now gone, replaced by The British Library but at the time the only Tetley's pub in London, had bar billiards in the 1960s, a game which has since almost disappeared but is having a revival of late with pub leagues, especially in Sussex, Kent and Cambridgeshire for some reason, and a national competition. This can only be to the good. Playing in The Rising Sun we thought the whole thing to be rather gentlemanly. Big power shots were no use; they only sent the wooden mushrooms flying. It was all about delicacy and subtlety. Maybe that's what's lacking in electronic machines and pool tables.

The tenant of a pub in Derbyshire woke up one morning to find that his masters, the brewery, had been taken over by another, larger set of masters. Before long a visit was made by the new area manager, and his parting gift was a detailed plan of the pub. Our friend the tenant, a publican of long experience and tralatitious views, was instructed to have a think, mark on the plan where he would like the two new electric fruit machines situated, and post the plan back to head office.

He did this, and was telephoned by a puzzled area manager. The following conversation ensued.

'Hello, John? Brian here. Got your fruit machine plan, thanks.'
'Yes.'
'But you seem to have put them in the car park.'

The answer came from one of the customers, a fellow called Andy Long who, suffering under the classification of medallion man, had run in to bowl for the cricket team with his shirt unbuttoned to the waist, revealing a paint-tin lid on a string. He, a good footballer, suggested that fines should be levied for dirty thoughts. A flat fee of 50p was decided upon, regardless of the degree of secret mental lewdness. Any male person jibbing when an especially attractive and/or scantily clad and/or well endowed female came into the pub, would be deemed a person not fit and proper by his peers, and so the lifeboat continued to be far too heavy to float.

These little stories are meant to illustrate the difference between a pub and a mere bar, or a shop, or a servery of any other kind. The building, its fittings, its staff and its products for sale, all conspire to bring in the customers, and all together produce a phenomenon that will hold marrow competitions, set up cricket teams while barring any stars currently playing recognised cricket, be generous to the community of which it is such an essential part, and take such matters, very small as they might be in the great scheme of things, very seriously indeed.

Shop!

'It is not in the shopkeeper's interest that his customers should hang about taking up space once their shopping is done, so his display is designed to sell as directly, crudely and quickly as can be contrived. In a pub it is different. Subject to your good behaviour, you are welcome to stay and be served until the law decrees otherwise. This fairly obvious fact seems never to have dawned upon the average marketing man, who tries to apply to the relatively static drinking situation the sort of brash, instant appeal, which in the supermarket, is meant to stop a housewife in full cry. A pub is not a shop, and if it looks like one the customers may well react unfavourably.'

The Traditional English Pub, Ben Davis

Will the marketing executives responsible for huge and ugly beer founts, which crowd the bar and grow ever uglier and more huge, please take note? How many times have you, gentle reader, changed your mind about what you were going to drink, after walking into a pub and being persuaded by point-of-sale advertising? Such a phenomenon must be as rare as football referees changing their minds about penalty awards. And yet, footballers protest, and beer taps will soon reach the ceiling.

CHAPTER TWO

The Quality of Pubness is not Strained

… which is to say, it is not forced. It droppeth as the gentle rain from heaven in the sense that 'pubness' has evolved, through usage and abusage, with occasional proddings from interested parties but mainly through the wishes of the customers, as expressed by their continued willingness to be so, and as observed by those wise people who saw what was wanted and provided it.

There have been problems, mostly caused by business managers wanting to make more money out of an institution so well established and so part of the currents of life that nobody for a moment thought it could go anywhere but up.

As we have seen, the pub as we think of it is the result of centuries of slow development, and it would be unreasonable to suggest that pubs should now be frozen in any image we might have of them, which would usually be a nostalgic view to do with the time we first started going in them. Equally unreasonable would be the destruction of the result of that slow development for no better reason than to try to maximise profits, because the destruction of something that has evolved over centuries to fit its purpose is almost bound to be a mistake and the increased profits will not, usually, accrue.

Every pub goer has a tale of woe about a favourite pub, and every beer drinker will be happy to tell you all about the shocking decline in the quality and choice of beer compared to whenever. The causes of such tales can usually be traced back, either to enthusiastic reformers of some kind who thought they knew better and could improve on the aforementioned centuries of accumulated common sense, or to the relentless agglomeration of the brewing industry. Unfortunately, when pubs are ripped apart they can never be restored. When breweries disappear, they never reappear, and when beer is reformulated for the sake of cost and/or efficiency it never is de-reformulated. Let us deal with beer first.

The identity is not recorded of the person who originally suggested selling bottled beer on draught. Certainly it was not a beer-drinking customer who said, 'Let's filter and pasteurise draught beer, so it's not a living thing any more. If it's flat and dead, we can then transport it long distances and it will keep much longer – almost for ever, in fact. We won't need skilled bar staff to look

In Old Shanklin village, Isle of Wight, **The Crab Inn** remains, largely as The Crab Hotel was in the early 1900s, from the outside at any rate. Here is a pub for which chocolate-box lids and jigsaw puzzles were invented. A big going-over on the inside may have improved matters from the point of view of business efficiency but, say reports, at the expense of that shadowy, elusive, irreplaceable attribute called 'character'.

after it and serve it, and if we put it through a chiller and fizz it up with carbon dioxide, the customers will never notice.'

'Ah yes,' said the chairman, 'but what about local tastes? They might not like our beer in a far off land, and they might not have heard of us.'

'That's all right, Mr Chairman. We'll dumb down our beer so it won't offend anybody, and we'll advertise it on the telly. We'll be a national brand, like Omo washing powder and Vesta beef curry. See how the money will roll in.'

And so occurred the top-pressure, keg-beer revolution. Thankfully, the counter revolution, led by CAMRA and others, has prevailed. There is no more Watney's Red Barrel, no more Whitbread Tankard – no more Watney's or Whitbread, come to that, and all that remains is the dreaded smoothflow-style

> ### *Pub Rubbish Korner*
>
> Once upon a time, let's say around the early 1960s, there were hundreds of breweries serving their local areas with – if you took a national count – three or four thousand different beers. There was a very good reason for this. Beer didn't keep very long and didn't travel very far on the roads then available.
>
> Then two things happened. A motorway network was built, thus making possible rapid long-distance travel and supermarket chains, and the big breweries began pasteurising and filtering beer, to be served by means of pressurised gases. The national brands of beer were born, and advertised on telly.
>
> Anything which is meant to be bought nationally has to offend as little as possible. It needn't please enormously but must settle down as a lowest common denominator product. Even as the 'real ale' revolution swept the country in protest against Watney's Red Barrel and the like, the motorway network and computerised distribution systems still made national brands a possibility, and a thing much to be desired by breweries, now run by accountants and marketing executives, whose only ambition was to be bigger and bigger.
>
> If a bland, sweet, undistinguished product takes hold of the market, the market loses interest in it as a product. If there is no difference between beers, they become nothing more than a means of getting drunk. Beer is just stuff to pour down your neck. It's called binge drinking. Suddenly the city pubs have a big problem of a Friday and Saturday night, but the brewers don't.

of beer which, as a chilled, sweet but otherwise almost flavourless 'product' is meant to appeal to those who won't eat their Brussels sprouts and would otherwise drink lager.

Some years ago, about 1977, your correspondent was writing a corporate brochure for one of the major breweries, now a brewer no more. From the research, two days in particular stand out in the mind. The first began with a visit to a Victorian brewery, still at work then, in a medium-sized market town in south-east England. Oh, all right, it was Wethered's of Marlow. Inside the many-storeyed red brick building, the head brewer conducted his tour party of one, and a cheery chap he was, despite having had to assume the duties of the cask sniffer who was off sick. Said sniffer, being an elderly retired gent

In the valley below Monsal Head in Derbyshire runs the River Wye, which Sir Richard Arkwright, he of the water frame, saw as an ideal power source for a new mill, so he began building one. Much later, with a thriving community around the mill, there were many complaints from the workers about the poor housing, so a model village was built. As an afterthought, in 1902, a workers' club was added.

The mill is now a complex of apartments, the private village is public, and the club is **The Cressbrook** pub, with its sign telling the story.

doing it part time, was the last of the line and our brewer didn't know how he would be replaced.

The brewery was spotless despite its age, all wood and copper, and the only technology visible was a hydrometer for measuring the original gravity of the brews. There were long, slim sacks of hops, called pockets, and everywhere had a pervasive aroma of malt and yeast and, well, beer.

That was the morning's job for your correspondent. In the afternoon, a visit had to be paid to a new brewery not very far away, on the outskirts of a town previously noted for its hats and motorcars. This brewery looked like a part of the ICI works in Billingham that had been recently visited on another job, with great tortures of pipework and vast storage containers like giant silos. On the edge of the site there was a control room, reminiscent of a Bond movie, where men with white coats and clip boards wandered about, occasionally pressing a button or saying something into an intercom. As yet, there was no sign of any brewing tackle. It was explained that swimming-pool volumes of 'product' could be switched from this silo to that in an instant, with confirmation courtesy of coloured lights. But where, the innocent wanted to know, was the brewing done?

Reluctantly, because it was maintenance week and no brewing was actually being done at the minute, the guide took the guided one to what seemed like an aircraft hanger filled with unidentified flying objects. These stainless steel machines were the modern equivalent of the mash tun, with every aspect of

> Don't take my boy to the Talkies!
> It's puttin' ideas in 'is 'ead,
> 'E makes the most 'orrible faces,
> And sleeps with a gun in 'is bed.
> 'E uses outlandish American words,
> It's nothin' but 'bootleggers', 'babies', and 'birds'.
> 'E says I've an English accent
> An' it's not that I mind the snub,
> But I want my boy to be British,
> So take 'im with you to the pub!
>
> *Dreadful Ballad of a Talkie-Ruined Home,*
> Sir Alan Patrick Herbert, 1890–1971

their functions controlled remotely. The guide, with some effort, lifted the lid of one, to reveal a thousand cockroaches scurrying around inside.

Another day was spent interviewing the directors. The production director said that the new brewery had been built to meet the foreseen demand for draught lager. Your correspondent protested. Draught lager was a nothing beer. It would never catch on. On the contrary, said the production director. Already in Scotland it accounted for 40 per cent of beer sales and the same would happen in England and Wales.

Another protest was made. Scotland was a beer desert, like Norfolk. All they could get in Scotland was McEwen's Export and Younger's Tartan. No wonder they drank lager. The director smiled. Wait and see, he said, wait and see.

We've had beerness; what about pubness? Because a great many old pubs have that special quality called 'atmosphere', some of those functionaries responsible for refurbishing knackered pubs think that atmosphere can be created by adding oldness. They don't realise that atmosphere is much more to do with the way the space is divided and arranged, and so they knock the whole place into one big room, stick some fake beams to the ceiling, nail a few plastic cutlasses to the wall, frame some copies of old theatre bills and hang them on the wall beside the cutlasses, wire up the stereo speakers and wonder why there's no atmosphere.

Ben Davis was an architect who specialised in pubs, working through the 1950s, 60s and 70s, and he was one of the few not of such a persuasion. In his book *The Traditional English Pub*, he lays out an entirely different philosophy.

'One can imagine a pub which, other things being equal, would be ideal for everyday use: a labyrinth of loosely connected interior spaces, intersected by

The Laxfield Low House need not be imagined. It's a labyrinth all right, with some startling changes of level in floor and many well-rubbed surfaces. The one thing it doesn't have is a counter, modest or otherwise. You have to queue at the taproom doorway.

see-through partitions, equipped with alcoves and changes of level in floor and ceiling, indeterminate in plan shape; enclosed in warm-coloured, well rubbed, semi-lustrous surfaces, mostly of natural materials and gleaming glass; linked with the great outdoors by fleeting glimpses of the street or countryside; having pools of glowing light in mellow surroundings; not over-furnished, the tables, stools and benches of strong timber subtly formed, burnished by contact with generations of arse and elbow; fitted with a modest counter having a polished and moulded hardwood top.'

There are several key points here, the first being that a pub should have rooms, not a room, and it should be the kind of place where you have to ask where the gents is. This very notion of a labyrinth of loosely connected interior spaces, intersected by see-through partitions, equipped with alcoves was the subject of periodic attack in the mid/late Nineteenth Century by the Temperance Movement and those who held themselves to be the guardians of public morality including, sometimes, the government.

Such arrangements would encourage prostitution and/or non-professional immoral behaviour between working men and loose women. Also, if drinkers could not be seen and supervised, they would drink to excess, especially the women, because respectable women didn't go in pubs much, because they didn't want to be seen drinking. Magistrates, all men of course, were given powers to demand structural alterations when licences came up for renewal, if they thought that alcoves could become a danger to virtue and order. This was despite the fact that those magistrates very seldom saw cases of licensees allowing prostitution, or permitting their houses to be used by thieves and vagabonds, or other pub-related illegal activities such as gambling. Relative to the numbers of drinkers, they saw few cases of drunkenness too. The most common offence before them was likely to be serving out of permitted hours.

On that subject, incidentally, it is a common misconception that licensing hours came in with the First World War. They were indeed made much stricter then but had been in force long before, especially on Sundays. Turning Sunday almost into a non-drinking day had had a reciprocal effect on Saturday nights, when folk had their week's wages in their pockets, which in turn increased the do-gooders' protests and concerns.

The pub's interior, says Davis, should be of wood, glass, brass, and plaster painted in comforting colours. It should have windows. It should not have fluorescent lights. It should have a lived-in look and feel.

Ben Davis developed his overall architectural view into a set of detailed principles, which he used to deliver as a training lecture to any brewery staff who might one day have something to do with designing or refurbishing a pub or a part of a pub. We might wish that he had had a wider audience and that his principles had been enshrined in law.

1. Red and brown are the warm colours. Do not use blues, greens or pastel shades.
2. Pub exteriors should be bathed in warm, welcoming light. Warm outside suggests warm inside.
3. Never be tempted to sacrifice character for efficiency or ease of supervision. Clinical is efficient, but pubs are not clinics. Once you rip out the character, the hither and thither, the higgledy-piggledy, you can never design it back.
4. Lighting can create atmosphere but it must be varied. We want pools of light. Uniform, bright light kills atmosphere. By all means be brightly lit (but not fluorescent) in your shop window, the servery, but not in every corner of every room.
5. Do not erect an over bar. Find somewhere else to store your glasses. You do not want your bar to look like a letterbox.
6. Keep things clean and polished and sparkling.
7. Avoid the 'mother's front room' effect. You are welcoming, you offer comfort and friendliness, but you are a public house.

8. Don't crowd the bar counter with a plethora of taps and pumps, and leave room on the counter, and provide stools, so that people can drink at the bar.
9. Decoration is important but it must not be false. If you have period things from the pub's own period, keep them and restore them, but don't try to add history where there is none.

So, would you go in the opposite kind of pub? From the outside, it looks like an industrial unit but with no windows. It has a silly name, such as The Whores and Strumpet, or The Venus Fly Trap. There are bouncers on the door.

If they let you in, using their own private set of criteria, you find a large, rectangular room, high ceilinged, painted in lime green, ice blue and orange. The music alternates between rap, drum and bass, strangled cat, garage and filling station. It is so loud you could never hear yourself speak, and the bouncers refuse to turn it down. You have to ask them because there are no other staff.

The drinks come in plastic cups from vending machines, which offer only smooth, lager and alcopops in violent colours, also pies and crisps. The furniture consists of plastic stacking chairs and Formica tables with chromium legs. Formica, incidentally, as well as being a trade name, is a proper word meaning an ant or an abcess in a dog's ear.

On one wall is a vast TV screen showing football. The commentary is on full volume but you have to get close to hear it. On another wall, a similar screen shows pop videos.

Of course, no such hideous pub exists yet, and let us hope it never does, but elements of it do. You can easily find pubs with several of these features, and you can only wonder why.

There are quite a few Old Crows, a Scared Crow in West Malling, a Crow Trees near Skipton, a Cock Crow at Hebburn which, admittedly, is not quite the same thing, and just one **Crow and Gate**. The gate part of a pub name is usually to do with a nearby church – churches always have prominent gates – or a gate in the city wall or a toll gate. The explanation here is purely geographical; it's in the Poundgate district of Crowborough.

CHAPTER THREE

The Straightest and the Highest Pub Crawls

Not very long ago, were you to drive through any residential area of England, Northern Ireland and certain counties of Wales, at a few minutes before twelve on a Sunday morning, you would see front doors opening and men emerging therefrom. These men would turn in the same direction and walk purposefully. They were going to the pub, which would start serving at noon and stop at two.

Many of these men wouldn't be staying that long. Behind the door recently opened, apple sauce was being made, or mint was being chopped, or eggs, milk and flour were being whisked for the Yorkshires, and Sunday dinner would be at one or one thirty and he would be home for it.

There is no such enforced discipline now that pubs can open and close whenever the management chooses, which is a matter for regret in a way. Although some pubs do still close on Sunday afternoons, at three or four perhaps, few if any close at two as they used to. Perhaps that's a reason behind the decline of Sunday dinner.

Even so, whatever hour the management chooses, the question still remains: are our pubs opening and closing at the right time? Pubs to the east of the Greenwich meridian will be opening some moments behindhand. Noon will have come and gone for them before it reaches Greenwich. Pubs to the west will open slightly prematurely. The Speculation Inn near Pembroke is about 210 miles west of Greenwich which means, if it opens promptly on Greenwich Mean Time, it's actually opening about twelve minutes early.

> I was going home two hours ago, but was met by Mr Griffith, who has kept me here ever since. I will come within a pint of wine.
>
> *Letters to His Wife*, January 3 1708,
> Sir Richard Steele, 1672–1729

But lo, the old inn, and the lights, and the fire,
And the fiddler's old tune and the shuffling of feet;
Soon for us shall be quiet and rest and desire,
And tomorrow's uprising to deeds shall be sweet.

The Message of the March Winds,
William Morris, 1834–1896

In the Third Century AD, two upper-middle class Romans called Crispin and Crispinian, possibly brothers, took up Christianity and, against the general tide of things, decided to preach the Gospel in Gaul. They ended up in Soissons, in what is now the Department of Aisne, and set about their missionary work meanwhile learning the craft of shoemaking, so that they could support themselves and give shoes to the poor.

Brought before the authorities on the orders of the persecuting emperor Diocletian, they suffered various ordeals, surviving the rack, being cast into the river Aisne with millstones around their necks, and being put into a great fire. In desperation, the sub-emperor Maximianus had them beheaded.

After all that lot, it may come as a surprise to learn of several pubs called The Jolly Crispin, but this is because shoemakers, having adopted Crispin as their patron saint, became known themselves as 'crispins'. About a dozen pubs are plain Crispins, and one is Crispin and Crispianus, another name for Crispinian, near Rochester, which seems scant memorial when the latter went through the same tortures as the former.

The Crispin pictured is in Great Longstone, near Bakewell.

In South Shields the **Dolly Peel**, formerly the Earl Grey, commemorates a locally famous lady who lived from 1783 to 1857. She was a fishwife, smuggler, publican, poet, singer and storyteller, and a friend of the town's first MP Sir Robert Ingham. She went to the Napoleonic wars as a stowaway and came back as a well-respected Royal Navy nurse, whereupon she took up residence in Shadwell Street. The pub is in Commercial Road and has clearly not been there long enough for Dolly to have sung or recited in it.

If we are to enter a pub at opening time precisely, and/or come out of it at closing time, we can only do this on or very near the meridian in question. This rather confines our choices because, using the old county boundaries, the line only runs through central Sussex, the eastern edge of Surrey, a corner of western Kent in which Greenwich used to be, Essex, Hertfordshire, Cambridgeshire, the edge of Huntingdonshire, Lincolnshire and the seaward tip of the East Riding.

If you feel a pub crawl coming on, it will be a marathon, starting at Peacehaven, Sussex, perhaps at The Badgers Watch. There's a monumental obelisk on the cliff top marking the meridian, so you can see how near you are to the correct time. The line brushes past Lewes to the west but there'd be no

There is a fine stuffed chavender,
A chavender, or chub
That decks the rural pavender,
The pavender, or pub,
Wherein I eat my gravender,
My gravender, or grub.

The Chavender, or Chub,
Warham St Leger, 1850–c1915

Signs of Old Times: The Jack the Ripper

Here, the endangered life form is the pub itself and not the management. Such pubs, called Theme Pubs, appear and disappear with equal suddenness, like flowers in the desert. Not long ago there were no such things as theme pubs and soon there will be no such things again. They therefore offer a rare opportunity to observe a species from the very beginnings of existence to extinction.

A between-the-wars, redbrick pub on the newer side of town used to be The Slow Worm and Pikelet and, before that, The White Hart. All traces of previous lives have disappeared in its reincarnation as the haunt of the famous stomach slitter.

The main room, the Whitechapel 1888 Lounge, features contemporary theatre bills and taped music of the kind that the pub chain's marketing manager imagines was heard in Victorian East End music halls. So, to the strains of *Get me to the church on time* and 'Chas & Dave's Greatest Hits', female bar staff – mostly resting actresses – strut about, dressed as Nineteenth Century prostitutes with appropriate boils, scabs, suppurating sores, missing teeth etc. They approach male customers with a sassy walk, hand on hip and a toss of the head, saying, 'Fancy a nice pint, dearie?'

When it's time for a barmaid's break, a male member of staff, dressed in black cloak and top hat, will spread artificial blood all over while acting as if slashing her neck with an open razor. He'll then drag her off, calling after him, 'Clear that up, will you?'

In the Annie Chapman Bar, customers can don virtual-reality headsets and re-enact the ripping in question, selecting one of three roles: the horrid slasher, someone looking through the window or, of course, they can experience the last moments of Ms Chapman herself.

The Long Lizzie Stride Bar is done out like an old mortuary with waxwork bodies lying on marble slabs in various stages post mortem. When customers tire of the near-freezing temperature they can wander into the toasty warmth of the Catherine Eddowes Eaterama, where steaming hot joints of the day are offered in a slice-it-yourself carvery.

If you do fancy a nice pint, you have a choice of three microbrewery real ales: Marie Kelly Koff-Kure (ABV 5.8), Polly Nicholls Jugular Jangler (ABV 6.4) and Liza Pearl Pulmonary Drain (ABV 8.2).

> The manager, upstairs with his CCTV screens and instant computerised till read-outs and stock-level displays, will shortly move to HQ. There will be a big meeting at which the marketing and finance people will discuss the next re-theme; possibly Imperial Rome, Seaside Holidays, the War of Jenkins' Ear, Lost Tribes of the Amazon, The Trials of Oscar Wilde, or Birds of Prey. After a while even they will realise that the theme pub is one of the silliest notions anyone ever thought of.

harm in popping into town, to the pub called The Meridian, perhaps, or The Black Horse, which are not far off the purpose, and neither is The Five Bells at Chailey, followed by The Green Man at Horstead Keynes. You really need to be on the east side of East Grinstead but that doesn't seem possible pub-wise, and so you might try The Ship Inn in, funnily enough, Ship Street. Into Surrey, Dormansland is slightly east of our line but nearer than Lingfield, so there's The Plough, The Old House at Home and The Royal Oak.

The Brickmakers Arms, Crowhurst Lane End, is a little to the west, as is The Haycutter, Tanhouse Road, Oxted, but only by a second or two when travelling at 1,000 mph, which you are, roughly. Compensate by stepping over the meridian to the very slightly eastern side and The Carpenters Arms, Limpsfield Chart.

Our first and only pub to be spot on the line is the Botley Hill Farmhouse, a short way northwest of Titsey on the Roydon road. Only here can you be sure that opening and closing time is the time. At The Old Ship, Tatsfield, you're to the east again, but at The Coney, Wickham, you're almost on it, and in Kent. We're getting close to Greenwich now, but a stop in Lewisham seems reasonable, not quite on the line but almost, at The Jolly Farmers, perhaps, or The Rising Sun, or maybe The Ladywell Tavern.

In Greenwich, as close as possible to the Observatory and the meridian, is the oldest pub in the district, The Plume of Feathers. Over the river into old Essex, the line runs through Canning Town – the Princess Alexandra is almost on the spot, Plaistow – Victoria Tavern, West Ham – the Park Tavern Hotel, Leytonstone – The George. The A11 more or less follows our path, where it's called Hollybush Hill, Woodford and Epping High Roads so, as the strawberry said to the raspberry, pick your own anywhere along there, such as The White Hart, which is very close. At Waltham Abbey, The Volunteer on Meridian Way is closer than The Woodbine.

Aristotle and many after him believed that dew fell from the sky like rain, a proposition difficult to understand as nobody then or since ever saw dew fall, because it doesn't. The book of Deuteronomy (no, really) had it right when it used the word 'distil' about dew. It is formed when a warm thing, a good radiator but a poor conductor, such as a blade of grass after a sunny day, gives off its heat in the still, clear night to the point where it is cooler than the surrounding air and earth. At this point, called the dew point, the atmosphere must give up its moisture to the cooler object, the blade of grass.

The other sort of dew is formed by leaves themselves as part of their normal lives. Those drops, like the one on the sign shown, are usually larger and are mostly leftovers from the day's moisturising activities by the plant's irrigation system.

The pun on 'Do drop in' is obvious and reasonably amusing, which is why there are ten such inns around the country. This one is in Hathern, near Loughborough, which used to have a different sign showing the drop about to fall from a tree onto a flower below.

Into Hertfordshire and, by the banks of the River Lee, The Jolly Fisherman at Stanstead St Margarets is but a longish cast from our way, and more hilarity is promised at The Jolly Bargeman on the eastern side of Ware. Now on the A10, on a part thereof once known as the Great North Road, is The White Horse at High Cross, very close, and The Sword in Hand at Westmill, and The Black Bull and The Fox and Duck are near as dammit in Buntingford.

According to the 1840 Pigot map of Hertfordshire, The White Bear in Royston is close enough for the pub crawl. It's on Kneesworth Street, that the Romans called Ermine Street that turned into the Great North Road aforesaid, before the southern A1 took on the job and before roads were thus classified, heading off for Huntingdon and joining the rest of the A1 at Wansford. Meanwhile, you can jostle the meridian there, or at The Green Man or The Boar's Head, both on Market Hill, although the two High Street pubs in Melbourn, The Star Inn and The Dolphin, are closer as we move into Cambridgeshire.

The Chequers at Orwell could be your next mooring, but not The Trinity Foot off the A14 south of Swavesey, unless a brave optimist has reopened it. The White Swan, Bluntisham High Street, is nearer the line than The Prince of Wales but briefly into Huntingdonshire in Somersham, a village that straddles the line, The Black Bull has to be on the list.

North of that are only fens, so back into Cambridgeshire but still fens, and into Lincolnshire where The New Saracen's Head, in the parish of Saracen's Head in the Hundred of Holland Elloe, a short distance north west of Holbeach, is not as near as we'd like but it's been a long way since The Bull. The east side of Boston, however, is pretty well on it, and The Mill Inn on Spilsby Road is close indeed. The Plough and Dove by the A16 in Stickney is also a little to the east and so is The George and Dragon in the splendidly named village of Hagworthingham, but by rather less.

The Lincolnshire Poacher, Eastgate, is on the right side of Louth. North of that is The New Plough, Covenham St Bartholemew, and very close to our line. The Crown and Anchor and The Fleece, at North Cotes, have to be the last in Lincolnshire for we must cross the water to the East Riding.

The Hildyard Arms and The Holderness are in the centre of Patrington, which is a little to the west but we are fast running out of possibilities. Roos is to the west of the point where the meridian crosses the English coast but there is a pub there, The Black Horse, and The Roos Arms if it's been reopened. Otherwise the only option is the residents' bar at the Sand-le-Mere static caravan site by the beach near Tunstall. Maybe it would be better to do this crawl the other way around, starting by hanging around the caravan site until someone agrees to take you into the bar, and finishing on a higher note at Peacehaven.

Talking of higher notes … the Pennine Way is just under 270 miles from The Old Nags Head in Edale, Derbyshire, to The Border Hotel, Kirk Yetholm, Berwickshire, or slightly further if you start at The Rambler Country House, Edale, which used to be called The Church. You get a free drink at The Border Hotel if you've walked all the way, but normal payments apply at the many other pubs on route and, if you're walking, oft-times you'd be glad of beer at twice the price.

At first, the Way is short on pubs and long on bog-hopping but, if you get lost in the mist and rain and come down from Kinder Scout too far to the east, you can look in to The Snake Pass Inn, on the A57 Manchester-Sheffield road, but you'll have a lengthy walk, four or five miles, to get back on track.

Knock, knock, who's gone where?

Many people lament the disappearance of the public bar, assuming perhaps that it has been a consequence of pub owners wanting to increase space, and/or of the populace's general move upmarket, and/or of the dissolution of the class system – rich man up at The Castle Inn, poor man down at The Creaking Gate.

While it may be true that the proletariat and the bourgeoisie are no longer so easily distinguished at a distance, an important reason for the decline of the public bar lies in our government changing the law without fully understanding the consequences (nothing new there, then), mixed with brewery short-sightedness.

Until 1964, a licence to sell beer, wines and spirits, called a Full On Licence, could only be granted to pubs with at least two rooms. Single room pubs could only get a beer and wine licence. At this time also, prices in the public bars were regulated and kept low, but not prices in other bars.

From 1964, when full on licences could be had for one-room pubs, a brilliant idea began occurring to pub owners, the great majority of whom were brewers. Why, if we knock this two- or three-room pub into one big room, it will no longer have a public bar. We can charge what we like.

Some wise magistrates insisted on the public bar being kept. Most didn't. Down came the walls, down went the carpets, up went the prices. If the pub was naturally hither and thither in construction, it might still keep its atmosphere and multiplicity of areas despite losing its partitions. If not, it became a large void, and a mainstay section of the clientele might go elsewhere.

Your middle classes, suddenly thrust against a dominant force of rude mechanicals, repaired to The White Hart Hotel. Or, your workmen, suddenly finding themselves surrounded by toffee-noses in suits, decamped to The Railway. Many pubs, with one bar double the size as the dust settled, found it hard to make up the loss of half their customary traffic.

Some suits had always and deliberately used the public bar. Some more salty types went in the saloon, provided they weren't in their overalls and boots. That had been their choice, but now there was no choice. Something had gone missing from our pubs and, like the settles ripped out of the old country inns, it will not be put back.

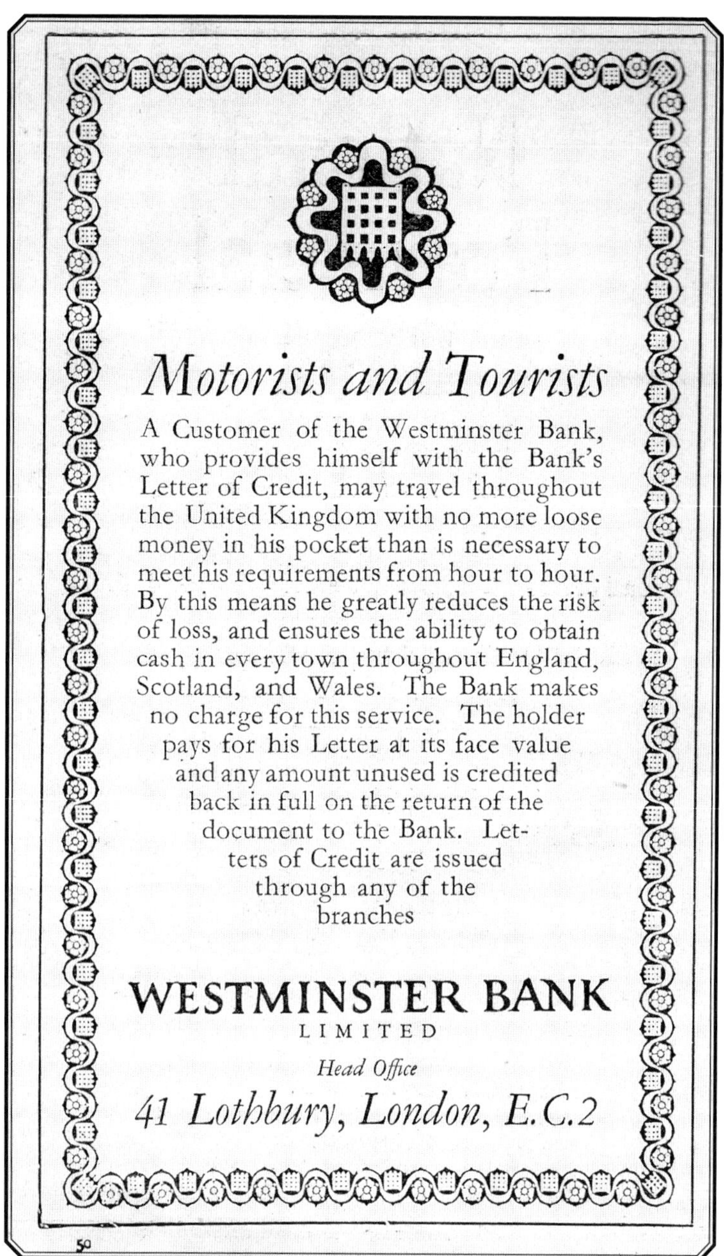

You might have needed this on the highest pub crawl had you been doing it in 1926. The pubs were all there then but there were no holes in the wall, and no Pennine Way come to that, and so if you'd tried to walk it you would probably have been shot by a gamekeeper.

> Let the world wagge, and take mine ease in myne inn.
>
> *Proverbes*, John Heywood, 1497–1580

Detouring the other way takes you towards Glossop, and the first pub you'll meet will be The Royal Oak, also on the Snake.

It is a trial of the spirit that the least pleasant, or should we say by far the most unpleasant part of the Way, has the fewest opportunities for a pint. Over Bleaklow, Black Moss and White Moss, there are no pubs that do not involve a substantial detour, and the best method of dealing with this is to get your head down and plough on for Standedge, where stand The Great Western and The Carriage House, not far from each other on the good old A62.

No detour at all is necessary for The White House on Blackstone Edge, a couple of miles after you've passed the Windy Hill transmitter and crossed over the M62 on a fine footbridge.

No Comment in London

'On the crest of Denmark Hill, just beyond the new King's College Hospital, stands the Fox-under-the-Hill, a well favoured tavern reminiscent of a House of Entertainment, and the headquarters of the Camberwell patrol when Dulwich and Upper Sydenham were infested by footpads and highwaymen; also of cross-country coursing with the hounds housed on the neighbouring Dog Kennel Hill. Today a stuffed fox in a show-case and a mere name instead of a sign are all that remain to recall its bygone associations.'

More London Inns and Taverns, Leopold Wagner, 1925

The Fox under the Hill was certainly there in 1786, seemingly a fairly remote, rural wayside inn at that time, but it is there no more, replaced a short distance further down the slope by The Fox on the Hill, a large pub in between-the-wars, Bayko Building Set redbrick, now a J D Wetherspoon's. There is another Fox under the Hill, on Shooters Hill Road, Woolwich, an Eighteenth Century pub refitted to suit 'the Hungry Horse concept' and offering five plasma screens, two pool tables, five types of lager and a 'smoking solution'.

You have choices when you approach Stoodley Pike. Do you take a shortcut down into the Mankinholes valley to visit The Top Brink Inn, Lumbutts, and then walk into Todmorden town where there is plenty of choice? Or do you go on to the pike in question, shortcut again into the main Calder valley and turn towards Todmorden to visit the Rose and Crown and on into town? Or, do you

There appear to be two eel's feet, one on the Norfolk Broads at Ormesby, near Great Yarmouth, which had a chef's head on its sign at the last time of looking, and this one in the very small village of Eastbridge, near Leiston and Sizewell, Suffolk.

In pre-hop days, the herb *Glechoma hederacea*, that we call ground ivy, was used in ale-brewing to help clarify and improve the keeping qualities of the ale, hence the other names for the plant of alehoof and tunhoof. The hoof part of the word is nothing to do with the ends of horses' legs but rather is from the Anglo-Saxon *hofe*, meaning … you'll never guess … ground ivy. There are no reliable references to this term alehoof ever morphing into alefoot, and why would there be, and so to say it was then doubly corrupted into eel's foot, as has been stated elsewhere, seems to be stretching things a bit.

One explanation of the name is that it's not an eel but a De'il, as a local holy man is supposed to have caught the Devil in a boot and thrown him in the sea. The same story is told of a Fourteenth Century rector in Buckinghamshire, Sir John Schorne, and there used to be a pub in Winslow, Bucks called The Devil in the Boot. Doubtless the same story is told of others in local and foreign parts.

If the name is based on a folktale, one can understand a certain superstitious reluctance to name the devil on an inn sign, although others do it. Why it's **The Eel's Foot** and not The Eel's Boot is not explained, nor is it clear why we always want to find rationality behind pub names. Maybe somebody just thought it was an amusing name for an inn in a village on a river near the sea.

follow the Way and turn off into Hebden Bridge? You have many options here too, perhaps starting with The Fox and Goose.

Back on the Way less than two miles will bring up The New Delight, and another three or so finds The Pack Horse at Widdop, and nothing more until Cowling, where The Black Bull Inn, on the Way, is reported closed at the time of writing and so a short walk eastwards along the Keighley Road may be necessary for The Bay Horse.

'Pleasant', 'bland' and 'unremarkable' are epithets applied on pub websites to The Hare and Hounds in Lothersdale. Ah me and lackaday, and lamentations for past years, about 40 of them. Having walked fifteen miles from The Pack Horse at Widdop, we found The Hare and Hounds in glorious evening sun. Like so many old village pubs then, it was bare boards and basics, which was exactly what we wanted.

Several pints had to be sunk before we could bring ourselves to ask about food. He didn't cook anything, the landlord said, but we were welcome to a sandwich. We, innocents abroad, were about to ask about the sorts of sandwiches, and we may even have thought about asking how much they might be, but he spared our shame by pre-empting us with a beckoning finger. We followed him behind the bar into the pantry. Flagstone floor, whitewashed walls, and pine shelves two-inches thick. On the broadest of these stood a massive oval carving plate, and resting thereon was most of a whole ham.

This was not a ham from a modern racing pig, but a ham from a happy pig that had lived a full life. The fat on it was three fingers thick. There was also a dish of mustard, and a great lump of farmhouse butter as big as a house brick and the same colour as the mustard. A crock was full of new floury loaves of crusty white bread, and a sweet jar was full of home-pickled onions.

The landlord pointed at this unimagined glory, and at plates and cutlery, and at a bone-handled carving knife that must have been his grandma's, so thin and sharp was the blade, and went back into the bar room. We were to help ourselves, and we did. My companion Jim, who had been to public school, suddenly came out with something from the Bible. 'In this mountain shall the Lord of hosts make unto all people a feast of fat things, a feast of wine on the lees, of fat things full of marrow.' He said he'd had to write it out a hundred times for complaining about his school dinner and had never forgotten it.

We went back to our table bearing our feasts of fat things, and the landlord wasn't there. There'd been a sharp shower earlier and he was sitting outside on a wooden chair, looking at the rainbow.

There are two pubs called **Eureka**, one in Ormskirk, and this one in South Shields which is built to an early Twentieth Century format recognisable to anyone familiar with working-class urban boozers. The sign depicts the sage Archimedes but not at his eureka ('I have found it' in Greek) moment of leaping from his tub at the public baths and running home naked, having had the thought which led to his Principle. As every schoolchild over

the age of 11 used to know, the said Principle states that when a body is immersed in a fluid, the apparent loss of weight is equal to the weight of the fluid displaced.

Before his bath, he had been trying to work out a method of testing the King of Syracuse's new crown to see if the goldsmith had substituted silver for some of the royal gold supplied. Now, having eureka'd, all Archimedes had to do was get hold of the exact same amount of pure gold the king had given the goldsmith, and compare its displacement with that of the crown. Since gold was the heaviest metal then known, if the crown displaced more water, because it was bigger having been adulterated with a lighter metal, the goldsmith was for the high jump.

Certain spoilsports at the university have pointed out that even if the goldsmith substituted a third of the gold with silver in the biggest crown then known, the difference in the amount of displacement would hardly be measurable. They do this, instead of trying to discover what happened to the goldsmith, which we'd much rather know about.

On the pub sign, Archimedes seems to be designing a siege engine, something he also did but which would never have made him cry 'Eureka', since he believed that applied science was an inferior trade compared with pure mathematics.

By the way, should you ever be in the pub and want to show that you know pi to thirteen decimal places, learn this, add three point at the front, and count the letters of each word: O that I could recollect of circle round, the exact relation Arkimedes found.

Long time passing and it was a Sunday lunchtime next time I was there, at The Hare and Hounds. The car park was full of expensive motors and the carpeted, music-piped bar was populated by the young sons of gentlefolk and their glamorous female companions. While the boys talked about the relative merits of GTis, XR3s, XTGs and all sek mak o' tackle, the girls in their short skirts and tight tops tried and failed to look interested. There was no point in asking about the wonderful fellow who used to have the pub, so I just had the one pint and left.

There's no pub in Thornton-in-Craven but you could divert to The Tempest Arms at Elslack, or just keep going to Gargrave where The Masons Arms is on your left on Marton Road, The Old Swan is on your right on the High Street, and The Anchor's a bit more of a step to the west, near the Leeds-Liverpool canal on Hellifield Road.

It was in Gargrave that I had a badly swollen ankle. A visit to the chemist's shop found a quite elderly lady from a recently bygone age, who went in the back for a minute and came forth with a bottle of grey water. 'Lead and opium,' she said. 'That'll fill the bill.' I can't remember what she charged but it was very little. We walked out of town and I poured the grey water onto the ankle, soaking my sock in it. The swelling seemed to decrease as I performed the act. By another mile it had gone completely. Lead and opium would be illegal today, I'm sure, and may well have been then, but it worked very much better than anything now on the market. I heard later that the old girl had walked out of her shop one day and been knocked down and killed by a motorcycle.

Next village is Airton but no pub, so on another mile to Kirkby Malham where is The Victoria Inn, and two more miles to Malham and you come first to the famous Buck Inn, and a few yards further on your right, in Finkle Street is The Lister Arms. Opinions are divided over which is the better hostelry so a visit to both is essential.

Nothing now for a day's march to Horton-in-Ribblesdale for The Crown Inn and The Golden Lion. It's about fifteen miles to the next pub, in Hawes, but during those miles you will pass the century, assuming you have kept to the route. Hawes, the chief town of Wensleydale and home of the eponymous cheese, makes things very easy for the pub-crawler. All four pubs, The Board, The Crown, The White Hart and The Fountain, are scattered around or very near the market square. Another mile and a half or so takes you to The Green Dragon where you might happen upon the brass band festival held in the natural amphitheatre behind the pub, where also tumbles Hardraw Force, a tall (for England) waterfall which, depending on recent rain, can be an impressive torrent or a pathetic dribble. In any case, you absolutely must not walk around behind it, although it is easy to do so, but no, you really mustn't.

When the King was Head Brewer

Early in the First World War, a problem became apparent in the munitions industry. Production at the massive new factory in the Scottish borders, at its peak employing 25,000 people, was suffering because of drunkenness among the workforce, many of whom were single men and women living in digs in Carlisle.

The answer was a radical one. The State took control of every aspect of the licensed trade in that city and surrounding district – brewing, pubs, off-licences, the lot. They closed almost half the pubs and all the off-licences, and prohibited advertising of alcoholic drinks. Strict regulations were enforced on opening times and sales to young people, and those pub managers directly employed by the government were given commission on food and soft drink sales but not on alcohol.

The Scottish custom of having a whisky chaser with your beer was banned, as was round buying. Prices were set across the whole estate, so no pub could encourage business by price cuts and, masterstroke of masterstrokes, they made the beer weaker. No other beer was permitted.

Drunkenness was indeed much reduced but, when that lousy war was over, there was a debate about what to do with the King's brewery. It was decided that it would operate like any other brewery, to make money, so they got on with brewing better beer, building new pubs and forgetting about their original purpose. One good principle remained: prices were kept low.

The good folk of Carlisle were very happy and, after the Second World War, the Labour government wanted to extend the scheme, but in 1951 the Tories got in and that was all forgotten about until 1971, when it became apparent that the business was a lot of work for not much reward, and so it was sold off.

Your correspondent's first visit to Carlisle happened to be at this time, and so one can bear witness to the passing of a unique experiment, started for warlike reasons, and the impression remains of basic, no-nonsense pubs selling excellent, distinctive beer. According to report, the majority of those who remember the King's beer, by then the Queen's beer of course, regret its passing and that of the pubs, so we can only join in with an expression of sympathy.

A publess trudge of nine miles brings you to Thwaite, where there is no pub but a diversion, three miles there and back, offers you The Farmers Arms at Muker. No civilisation at Keld either, only a youth hostel, but beckoning a mere four miles away is the highest pub in England, and so obviously the highest on our crawl, at Tan Hill, 1,732 feet above sea level. This is the pub with no locals; nobody lives near it and hasn't done since the coalmines closed that it was built to serve. In fact, until the 1930s it was named after the main mine, the King's Pit.

Arriving there by chance on the day of the Tan Hill Sheep Show, Jim and I put up our tent – the soil is very thin on rock, so bring extra pegs – and joined in the post-Show festivities. The pub seemed to be entirely filled with very large, red-faced men wearing huge tweed jackets. Every time one of them stood up, his jacket swept several pint glasses off the table onto the floor. They said 'By' all the while, so if you closed your eyes you could think you were in a room full of sheep.

The Tan Hill used to have a reputation for being unreliable as regards opening; on another occasion your correspondent, having reached it on foot after a very, very wet day from Hawes in October to find it boarded up, can vouch for this. In more recent times, although it's liable to be snowed in during winter months, you have always been able to find it open at a reasonable hour.

Bowes is next, now bypassed by the A66 but still offering a fine coaching inn at the sign of The Ancient Unicorn. Never was a pub more welcome than that October time, after striking on past the Tan Hill for the next seven miles, making it 24 in the day, all in pouring rain and the last half dozen in the dark of night, following a vague guess at our line through the morass that is the valley of the Sleightholm Beck. Showered, in dry clothes, drinking beer in the Unicorn while they cooked our supper, we read in one of the guide books that on no account should anyone stray into that desolate area in bad weather, but rather take the road.

Bowes to Middleton-in-Teesdale can be done in a long, hot, sunny morning, even with a heavy pack. I know this because, in the days of two o'clock Sunday closing, after such a morning, Jim and I looked down on the bridge over the Tees at a quarter to two. Jim, being of semi-noble birth, was not going to run but I certainly was, carrying 60 pounds on my back or no. With six pints drawn at The Bridge Inn, by an amused landlord for an exhausted short-distance but handicapped runner, Jim strolled in at one minute to two and quietly and, I hope, secretly gratefully, sank his ration. The other pub is The Forresters, on the square, equally a saviour on another occasion when B&B was required.

The Fat Ox in Whitley Bay is not to be confused with The Durham Ox, a beast of the early 1800s that toured the country in a specially constructed waggon and had about twenty pubs named after it, including The Ketton Ox at Yarm as it was bred at Ketton, Co Durham.

The Whitley Bay ox was earlier, and the original pub, rebuilt in the 1920s, was named shortly after the ox was walked to market from a farm near Whitley Bay to Newcastle, a distance of nine miles or so, over a period of seven days in 1789. Whitley Bay, by the way, was also home to Gladstone Adams, photographer, early motorist and aviator, who has no pubs named after him despite inventing the windscreen wiper.

Middleton to Holwick is about three miles, where stands The Strathmore Arms, which may be closed on a Monday, after which The High Force Hotel and, a little less than a mile off the Way, The Langdon Beck. It's actually a good diversion because the Way proper takes you around the foot of Widdybank Fell along the bank of the Tees, whereas a more interesting thing to do is to walk up from the Langdon Beck to Cow Green reservoir and down the side of that to Cauldron Snout. It's quite a long step to the next refreshment but there is compensation at High Cup Nick, one of the most astonishing sights in England. On a clear day you can see the Solway Firth, many of the Lake District peaks, and the Howgills to the south, while below you spreads a blessed green valley.

At your next lowest point lies the village of Dufton and The Stag Inn, a pub once reminiscent of an impoverished dentist's waiting room in rural Uzbekistan, and selling only cold fizz, but now greatly, greatly improved. Recitation by heart of the anonymous lines below, in the correct accent, may get you a free pint, or not.

Ode to Dufton

> Thoo's nivver eerd o Dufton?
> Why, weer's ta lived afoor?
> It ligs reet under Dufton Pike.
> Thoo'll seet frait auld barn door.

Translation for Southerners: You've never heard of Dufton? Where have you been, for goodness sake? It lies right under Dufton Pike. You'll see it if you're near enough.

> It's a gay queer spot is Dufton,
> Ant fwoak inside ana.
> Ther terble independent, like,
> An ard as that stean wa.

Dufton is a very strange place, and the people there are a good match. They keep themselves to themselves and resemble a stone wall in obduracy.

> If thoo ivver gaas ti Dufton,
> Thoo'd bitter mind thisel.
> Thoo'd nivver see thi at agin,
> If twind's bloan straight offt fell.

Prime contender for the most often used pub name, the heraldic red lion of John of Gaunt, and of King James I and VI, advertises the presence of over 650 pubs. Although there are almost twice as many crowns if you include the ones with roses, sceptres, cushions, anchors and so on, there are also twice as many lions if you include the black, the golden and all the others. Of plain The Crowns, there are but 500, and so **The Red Lion** has it.

This one, photographed in 1929, is at Avebury, a very big pub for a very small village, but it is central to the standing stones and is supposedly haunted by at least six ghosts, including that of a young wife who took a lover while hubby was away at the Civil War. He came home, found her in flagrante delicto, shot the lover and ran her through, dropping her body down the well. The top of the well is now in one of the bars and Florrie, for that was her name, will emerge from her watery grave should a man with a beard walk past it.

The building is Sixteenth Century but wasn't turned into a pub until the turn of the Nineteenth. It still looks much the same from the outside as it did in 1929 although not offering tea rooms any more.

Should you ever visit Dufton, you would be well advised to take care. You might lose your hat if the Helm Wind is blowing.

> Ther nin si daft at Dufton
> If yan's gitten owt ta sell.
> Ooivver, tho mun larn like me.
> Ah's nut inclined ta tell.

Beware of Duftonians offering goods for sale. Still, I had to find that out for myself and so will you.

> It'st bonniest spot int coonty
> Fer a it stans si hee.
> Aye, an visitors i'undreds,
> Gaas theer way up frait sea.

It's the prettiest place in Westmorland, despite its excessive altitude. For proof of that, count the tourists who come from Workington and Maryport.

> Yon pike sis varra laal frai ere
> But just thoo try ta clim.
> Afooer lang yar's oot o puff
> Ant sweat runs off thi chin.

Looking up at the pike, it may seem very small, but try to go up it and it will render you breathless and wet.

> By gum but wan yar gits tat top
> If'ts owt sek like a day,
> Thoo'll see fer ower thetty mile
> Aye, an vanner ivvery way.

The view from the summit, on a clear day, stretches for over thirty miles in almost every direction.

> Oh aye ther varra dyeacent fwoak
> An terble kind as weel.
> Oor lass she co frai Dufton toon
> An that ses quite a deal.

For all that, Dufton people are generous and honest. My wife is from Dufton, and I have very good taste.

> I Dufton kirk, ya Whi Sunder,
> At hoaf past yan bit clock,
> We tweea war wed amang oor frens
> Frai Dufton an frai Knock.

We were married at Dufton church, at 1330 hours on Whit Sunday, in front of guests from as far away as Knock.

> Thoo mun git a lass frai Dufton,
> An deea as weel as me.
> Shil mak a soarts o stuff ta eat
> Like berry kyeak fer tea.

You should follow my example in the matter of wives. They're all good cooks in Dufton, and especially talented when it comes to fruit cake.

> Apple dumplins an roobab tarts,
> Yearb puddn, pease puddn an sek,
> Wi traykle taffy an brandy snaps
> An yam med wine ta lep.

Not to mention various other delights, to be taken with homemade wine.

> Ah mind ya clashy winter's neet,
> Twas stoor an drife an a …
> But gaa an git thi ten o'clocks!
> Ah dunt tell a ah knah.

I remember one wild winter's night, with fog and a stormy … but hey, it's time for elevenses. I've said all I'm going to.

It's a day's march up and across the highest Pennine, Cross Fell, along the east-west watershed where the Tees starts one way and the tributaries of the Eden go the other, and down to the tiny village of Garrigill, where The George and Dragon awaits. At the time of writing, it had been forced to close after two years of poor trading, but reopened due to popular demand and a Save The Dragon campaign. However, the current intention is not to open every day.

Signs of Old Times: The Surly Old Git

Of all the unholy crimes committed by accountants and marketing executives, the decimation of our pubs and publicans is possibly the most odious. The Ye Olde Hayemayker Inne chain has 500 exactly similar pubs, serving smoothly flowing 'beer' at Arctic temperatures, plus Tyme Honoured Fayre cooked and frozen hundreds of miles away, all served to the accompaniment of a repeating Kylie Minogue CD. These are managed houses, doubtless excellent in their own way, but they are not the right places for sighting those increasingly rare, distinctive and endangered creatures, the Proper Landlord and Landlady. These pillars of the community can only be found in the increasingly rare, distinctive and endangered types of pub they oversee.

Not long ago, pub keepers were often retired from another trade. Wing Commanders, business executives, journalists and footballers all thought they could run a pub and often they were right. The pub business is not so easy now. Fewer Wingcos and no footballers want to do it. The lifetime pub professional in a free or tenanted house is also disappearing. One day, all pubs will be run by head-office trained managers, which will mean no more room for individuals, such as we find in The Surly Old Git.

One or two people come from miles around to try to chat with the character who keeps this time-capsule, hidden away on the canal bank, mid city, between the back of the Hospital for Tropical Diseases and the Yeung Chow Chow Fan Wholesale Warehouse.

The Surly Old Git is exactly as it was when its purpose in life was to cater for the eager, laughing crowds coming off shift from the drop forge, but today's customers, mostly journalists, are there in the hope of witnessing a Heritage Moment, when a stranger walks in and catches one of the last, genuinely baleful glares left in the British leisure industry. The facial expression they are waiting for should have its own brown sign on the motorway.

Infallibly, it is induced in the eponymous landlord by a new and insensitive customer's recitation of the following lines:

'Ah, mine host! A foaming pint of your finest draught mild, if you would be so kind. Very well then, I shall have bitter. Yes, the smooth will be fine. And a spritzer for my good lady here. Dry white wine and soda. Ah, right, well, a cider would be excellent. Or, indeed, as you say, a half of smooth. And what flavour crisps do we have this fine day? Two packets of pork scratchings, of course. Could you just top that pint up for me, please?'

From The George and Dragon it's only four miles to Alston, highest market town in England at 1,000 feet above sea level, a title also claimed by Buxton, also at 1,000 feet in Derbyshire. Which town has the last inch depends on where you stand, but Alston market is dead and gone while Buxton only shrinks and is on twice a week. Four miles is quite enough for a gentle morning and, having had a hearty breakfast, one might feel a thirst coming on if the sun is shining. Wanting to get into the town centre, you might walk past the Victoria Inn and the Crown Hotel but you surely won't mind making a tiny diversion off the route to go into Alston market place and The Turk's Head.

The Geese Have Gone Over The Water, in the Hanover district of Brighton, was The Golden Cross not long ago, 30 years or so. The original Geese sign showed a sailing ship heading for the open sea, which at least suggests that the name is nothing to do with a native-American creation story in which a V formation of geese saves a goddess falling from the sky. What it does have to do with, remains a mystery, although the most convincing theory is that an Irish landlord, in converting The Golden Cross into a kind of Murphy's bar, was making reference to his own emigration from the Emerald Isle.

There are about 30 Grey Horses, predominantly in the coal-mining districts of the north and midlands, three times as many as there are Grey Mares, Old and otherwise. The grey mare was a reference to 'she who must be obeyed' or 'er indoors', and so we may guess that there was a landlady in this case who wore the trousers. The grey horses, at least where coal was the thing, were the packhorses, sturdy fell-pony types, the pre-railway means of taking coals to Newcastle and other centres of distribution.

There is only one **The Greys**, bang opposite The Geese Have Gone Over The Water, making two unique pub names in one street.

No more pubs now until Slaggyford. It was a hot, hot late afternoon when Jim and I walked into this Northumberland village. There was nobody about. The long single street was empty and silent. The map showed PH but we couldn't see it. We remembered arriving in Horton-in-Ribblesdale to find that the first of the PHs marked there had become a girls' school.

A door opened. A lady looked at us in that steady, warm but cautious way older village people have. We asked her where the pub was and she said she didn't think there was one. I looked at Jim and he looked at me. Oh no. We walked a hundred yards more and asked another lady who was doing a bit of weeding in her front garden. Oh yes, she thought there was a pub, down by the church at the far end of the village, but she doubted if it would be open.

A most unpromising detached building had a sign above the door proclaiming 'The Kirkstyle Inn and Sportsman's Rest'. The door was in the centre and it was open, with a large and filthy window on each side. Going in, we could see that the room on the left was entirely full of newspapers and milk bottles. Newspaper stacks reached to the ceiling. Unwashed milk bottles were everywhere there was space not filled by newspapers. We went into the room on the right, which had a few small tables and chairs but no bar.

A large, quite elderly man shuffled in from nowhere. He was wearing a grey worsted suit, which may have been of reasonable quality at some earlier stage but

Pub Rubbish Korner

Of the half dozen pubs named after Dick Turpin and the couple of dozen more that claim he stayed there, hid there, drank there, ate there or was born there, very few can have any real connection with the bungling but ruthless extortioner and cattle rustler, known largely for something he never did.

He did not have a horse called Black Bess and he did not ride from London to York in 24 hours to give himself an alibi. That was an episode from a novel, *Rookwood*, by one Harrison Ainsworth, 1834, based on a real ride by another, earlier criminal, John Nevison, in 1676.

The Blue Bell Inn, Hempstead, near Saffron Waldon, claims to be the robber's birthplace, but so does The Spaniards on Hampstead Heath where Turpin Senior is claimed to have been landlord. Dick's father was probably a farmer and publican and he probably had a pub called The Rose and Crown in Hempstead. The Blue Bell was once called The Rose and Crown, and there was a Richard Turpin registered as born in that parish in 1705. This evidence seems much more convincing than The Spaniards' story, which has no evidence at all to back it, especially as it wasn't a pub when little Dicky took his first breath.

Other sources wrongly say Epping is the birthplace, where the oldest pub is The Black Lion, which also 'is reputed to have connections with Dick Turpin'. There may well be connections, not with his birth but with his Epping Forest period.

The Dick Turpin in East Finchley has a loose sort of association, being on what used to be Finchley Common by one of the main roads north (not the Great North Road, which in those days began with the modern route of the A10). Such a hostelry may well have been much frequented by thieves and vagabonds like Turpin, although there is nothing to say that the man himself was one of them.

The Dick Turpin in Newcastle-under-Lyme is on Gallows Tree Lane but Dick never went there. He did live at The Ferry Inn in Brough, East Yorkshire, and was arrested there, but most of his inglorious career was spent around Epping Forest and other parts of rural Essex. When things got too hot for him he removed to Yorkshire where he became John Palmer the farmer, often rustling stock rather than buying it at the auction mart. Eventually exposed as Turpin, he was hanged at York in 1739 and mostly forgotten about, until his life became Victorian legend.

now was struggling to do its job. Certainly the trousers had given in and, through the gaping fly, could be discerned a shirt tail of uncertain colour. A strange odour of mustiness accompanied this man like an aura. It reminded Jim and me of something very like the smell of old, damp newspapers and sour milk.

The man, whom we assumed to be the landlord of this pub, The Kirkstyle Inn and Sportsman's Rest, said nothing. Not even an eyebrow was raised to us in enquiry.

We asked for two pints of bitter. There was none.

Mild? None of that either. So what was there? There was some bottled Guinness. We ordered two of those and, having ascertained the suitability of the churchyard for camping, settled in for the evening. We had some sandwiches and pies for supper, bought in Alston, so we didn't need to cook, and there's always a tap in churchyards so we'd be all right for a brew.

Two more Guinness were followed by two more, and two more. That was four each we'd had. We asked for the same again, but we couldn't have it. There was now only one bottle left, and a man generally called by on his bicycle at half past nine for a Guinness, so that would have to be reserved for him.

Many years later, being near Slaggyford in the car, a call simply had to be made. The two rooms were one, with a long bar down the side and a juke box in the corner. There was a carpet on the floor. There were curtains at the spotless windows and specials on the board. Boring, but they had all sorts of things to drink.

Things get rather Roman for a while after Slaggyford. There's the Maiden Way, a Roman road high on a ridge, and Hadrian's Wall coming up. Before the Wall you can pop into the Greenhead Hotel. Following it, you can divert a short way to The Milecastle Inn, likewise further along to The Twice Brewed Inn. The legend is that a gang of building workers arrived at the inn in the 1750s and found the ale so feeble that they demanded it be brewed again. In 1934 the first UK youth hostel was opened nearby, the noble lady doing it being a strict teetotaller. She expressed the hope that the tea would be brewed but once, and so that name stuck to the non-alcoholic part of the village.

Heading more or less due north from the Twicey one can take photos of oneself and friends crossing Shitlington Crags, before arriving in Bellingham (pron. Bell-in-jum) where there are three hostelries; The Rose and Crown, The Black Bull and The Cheviot. Another fifteen or so miles brings you to the Byrness Hotel and that, my friends, is that. You have no choice but to cross the Cheviots, barren of everything never mind pubs, 27 miles of Scottish humps, each of which looks exactly like all the others, although your actual Muckle Cheviot is allegedly a few feet higher than the rest. And there, at last, is The Border Hotel, and if you've done those 27 miles in a single stretch, you surely deserve the free beer.

Who's behind the bar?

There are three basic business arrangements for pubs: owned, tenanted, managed. They can all be good, bad or indifferent because the success of the pub as a business depends, not on the type of arrangement, but on who are the key figures therein.

An owned pub, a free house, generally has its owner as landlord and, as it were, chief executive. Such a person can choose where to buy the drink, and can usually buy beer more cheaply than the tenant and so has a competitive advantage. Such a person can be a jolly good egg with a rosy-hued vision of running a pub as personal paradise, or a thoroughly sour and miserable, avaricious pig who should never have gone into the pub in the first place, or anything in between. The best ones combine humour and an understanding of the mission, with a sound business sense. That way, the pub stays busy and open.

Pub managers are on a salary. Unlike free-house owners, they are always experienced in the catering trade but, as in every walk of life, they vary. They don't have an interest in the fabric of the place and, annual bonus notwithstanding, may not have much interest in keeping up the trade. On the other hand, they might love the job. They might be consummate professionals who want to gravitate upwards, as they might see it, to pubs of their own one day, or to senior management in the company.

Tenants equally are a mixed bunch and getting more so, as breweries and pub-chain companies find it more and more difficult to recruit them, usually as a couple. Tenants pay a premium and a rent to the pub owner, possibly plus going-in money to the previous tenants, and are contracted to buy supplies from certain sources. In theory, between the rent, overheads and the wholesale cost of stock, and the retail prices over the bar, there is room to make a living. Experienced tenants will tell you that there is not so much room as there used to be, but the good ones in a pub with potential will always do nicely.

Here is an example of the figures a new publican must consider. It's the real thing, from an average-size country pub in a small village. It's thatched, old, with beams and open fires, several rooms – the perfect pub. There's a big garden where they hold the village fête. It could be a film set for *Midsomer Murders*.

To survive, it must attract trade from beyond its own parish, which basically means food trade. Although there are towns nearby, they have good pubs too, and restaurants. This pub is being offered as a tenancy by the brewery as we write because the previous tenant did a runner.

Beer trade has been steady at just under 90 barrels a year, which is not a lot. Wine trade is up, to almost 1,500 litres, minerals also up to 2,500 litres, but spirits are down to 90 litres. No figures for food. Ignoring normal overheads such as insurance and rates, the once-only going-in money for this pub will be about £30,000. Some of that will be recouped: it includes a deposit of £5,000, stock that can be sold, and F&F that can be sold on to the next tenant, assuming you don't do a runner too. Rent, payable fortnightly in advance, will be discussed at the interview.

Tenants, like free-house owners, can be terribly misguided when 'improving' their pubs. This one doesn't need improving. It is overflowing with pubness. What it needs is a good cook and a personable mine host or, as the advert puts it, 'would suit community minded applicants with strong catering and marketing skills'.

Or, as Ben Davis puts it in *The Traditional English Pub*: 'If the small rooms are sympathetically coloured and furnished the people will automatically feel secluded and can hardly avoid being sociable. When it comes to continuity, all one has to do in a genuine old building is firmly to exclude the more intolerable of the anachronisms inherent in the situation, and in such surroundings there is nothing to prevent the licensee's own brand of good-heartedness from permeating the scene.'

Finally, we have the bar staff. This is a very personal business. Personality and attitude are all important. Some bar staff think that selecting the next CD to put on the sound system is more important than serving a waiting customer. Some find it hard to leave the games machine to get back behind the bar. Some, despite being on minimum wage and having to make complicated arrangements for their young children, are absolutely brilliant.

CHAPTER FOUR

A Short Rant, and some Names

Every pub goer, city based or not, laments the decline of the country pub. Most of the old definition of what is necessary for a rural community – pub, church, school, shop with post office, village hall – no longer applies when almost everyone has a car to take kids to school, supermarkets are rarely more than a few miles away and the internet offers home delivery, hardly anyone goes to church and, most worrying of all for this (elderly) writer, fewer people are using the pub.

One of the oldest Stars, this one at Alfriston, between Newhaven and Eastbourne, is claimed to have been in business since 1450 or so, with the building going back 200 years before that. Usually, the star was that followed by the three wise men of the East, or it symbolised the Virgin Mary as *Stella Maris*, star of the sea. The Alfriston inn, originally run by monks as a hostel for pilgrims, was indeed The Star of Bethlehem.

Today's weary pilgrims can enjoy 'in-room treatments' given by qualified therapists. There is also WiFi, and duck liver and foie gras parfait, elements of hospitality not envisaged in 1450 or, for that matter, 1928 when our picture was taken.

There are at least 160 Stars, plus a great many Seven Stars, referring to the solar system or other astronomical configurations, North Stars, White Stars and even a Green Star in Smallthorne, Staffordshire.

Continuing our short tour of the student-ish regions of Brighton, we find a pub perhaps more aptly named for its clientele, **The Hector's House**. Modern students would not have seen the original broadcasts of the eponymous puppet show in the 1960s and 70s, featuring Hector the Dog and ZsaZsa the Cat, the latter voiced by a young and ultra-feline Joanna Lumley. Like *The Magic Roundabout* it was a French show, bought silent by the BBC and given narration and sound effects from whatever the pictures seemed to imply. Sound is a major component of the pub, too, much to the enjoyment of those who seek it as loud as possible.

Politicians, brewers and pub-chain tycoons are frantic, trying to work out what should be done to save the country pub. Seeing as the decline has been almost entirely their fault in the first place, perhaps they should be concentrating, not on doing, but on undoing. Politicians forced the large brewers to sell off thousands of pubs to management chains that are now going bust. They imposed the smoking ban. They devised a tax system that allows supermarkets to sell booze more cheaply than bottled water. They are taking a nuclear-powered sledgehammer to crack the city-centre nut of binge drinking, causing widespread collateral damage across the entire country while not affecting binge drinking in the slightest.

Time was when brewers saw their estate, their tenanted houses, simply as sales outlets. Brewers brewed and were pleased to have an assured local market. Publicans took the beer, sold as much of it as they could, ran the pubs as they saw fit and grumbled about the difficulties of getting any money out of the brewers for refurbishing the loos.

Tetley's was in Leeds, Watney's was in London, Harvey's was in Sussex, Thwaites was in Lancashire, Adnams was in Suffolk, Brain's was in south Wales, et cetera. There was no room in this arrangement for a third party and no need for it. Everybody knew what they were doing. There was no necessity for a team of highly paid people to investigate 'the quality of pubness', because everybody knew the answer. There was no need for marketing departments, personnel (sorry, human resources) managers, financial planners, directors of strategy, area managers, area managers' managers, and all the other suits and salaries now skimming the froth off the tenanted pub business.

Because these people have to be paid, the tied tenants' rent and 'going-in money' have to go up, so prices in pubs have to go up. When the tenants want a new loo seat or the front door repainted, they can't just ring up and get it seen to. There has to be a risk assessment procedure, a purchase department manager's approval, a purchasing director's approval of the manager's decision, an in-pub equipment quality facilitator to initiate the process, and a graduate trainee executive to go round and check if the pub really does need a loo seat or the front door painting.

Who's behind the bar?

In the days when keg bitter and draught lager were making their first unholy inroads into the sacred temples of real ale, someone wrote a fine poem:

> Not turning taps
> But pulling pumps
> Gives barmaids ample
> Breasts and rumps.

In these few words lay hidden the deep, agonising dread which the increasing popularity of pasteurised beer and lager brought about in the drinking man of that time. If it were no longer necessary to be versed in the arts of keeping and drawing live beer, and in holding one's own in the superior forms of repartee induced by real ale, then anybody could be a barmaid. You'd get college girls, or hitchhikers from New Zealand. Anybody. If barmaiding ceased to be a skilled trade and became a mere function, the end of the world was nigh.

It's all come true. Bar staff these days are invariably university graduates and/or Antipodeans. More than half of all pints sold are lager and many of the rest are the sterilised, homogenised, filtered, denatured, supercooled, smoothly flowing ersatz caricature of beer which the brewers have foisted on us, not because we asked for it but because they wanted to de-skill the brewing, carting, storing and serving process.

Soulless marketing managers and accountants thus not only made their deplorable mark on the British public house. They also consigned the Proper Barmaid to oblivion.

No Comment in London

'As a coaching inn the Angel was hardly superior to the Peacock, but it enjoyed pride of position with an ample forecourt at the crossways and had, moreover, a large music-room for the entertainment of travellers who, arriving from the North after dusk, rather than risk molestation by armed footpads, elected to pass the night at the familiar hostelry and seek their destinations in the full light of day. The same fears swayed the minds of ordinary Londoners and their Womankind who, at eventide, wandered up Goswell Street or the City Road on pleasure bent to the distant village.

The votaries of pleasure never considered the adventures of a night fittingly brought to a close without making the Angel their last house of call for a good supper. If, however, as was only too likely to happen, this had its full complement of feasters, the Peacock and the White Lion, or, across the way, the Blue Coat Boy and the White Swan, received the overflow. Of course we are here alluding to that happy-go-lucky age prior to the year 1873, when licensed premises were allowed to remain open until the grey dawn.'

More London Inns and Taverns, Leopold Wagner, 1925

The Angel Inn was rebuilt in 1899 with a cupola on top that has since become a famous landmark. It was translated into a Lyons Corner House in 1921 and eventually into a branch of the Co-operative Bank. J D Wetherspoon opened a pub next door and called it The Angel. There is a White Lion Street but no White Lion, and no Swans or Peacocks grace the distant village, nor boys from charity schools in their blue coats. The Old Red Lion, St John's Street, would now be the nearest house of call for votaries of pleasure in that district but they may have to go elsewhere if they wish to remain until the grey dawn. Ordinary Londoners and their Womankind could stop off earlier at The Pheasant in Goswell Road, and your correspondent and lady wife had their wedding reception at The Island Queen.

Meanwhile, tenants are tied to a contract that would be illegal anywhere else in the EC, by which the brewery charges them 50 pence a pint more than they charge everybody else, free trade and wholesale.

And, if they get through all that lot and increase their pubs' success, the more they do so, the more the rent goes up. And if, eventually, they give in and say sod it, the brewery directors will have trouble replacing them, and they will wonder why it is getting so difficult these days to find people who want to run pubs.

When the pub-owning chains bought up all that real estate, they thought they couldn't go wrong. They put managers in, did big deals with brewers to get the beer cheaply, had food cooked and frozen in central kitchens, printed standard menus, put bar staff on the minimum wage and waited for the money to roll in. Alas and alack, what with the politicians, the property market and that simple fact that there's no room for a third party, the chains are in the deepest trouble, refinancing and desperate to unload that which they bought at a silly price.

The consequence is, pubs closing at a rate that nobody, except possibly the old pub landlords, the old family brewers and the experienced pub-going public, could have prophesied.

And now, here are some of the most popular and, if we may put it thus, some of the more significant, pub signs, and the meanings and stories behind them.

No Comment in London

'Way down Wilton Place is another genuine bit of Old Knightsbridge utterly unknown to the average Londoner. Here Kinnerton Street, narrow and not unpicturesque, would reveal lodgings for single gentlemen, queer little shops of the village type, an altogether amazing number of courts and alleys with gossiping women and troops of children, in between small houses; two old-world taverns, the Nag's Head and the Horse and Groom, the Wilton Arms, established 1826 but recently rebuilt, and the Turk's Head at its junction with Motcomb Street, off Belgrave Square. As in Wilton Crescent Mews, the whole of the opposite side comprises stables and coach-houses which have been turned over to modern usage as depositories for horseless carriages.'

More London Inns and Taverns, Leopold Wagner, 1925

The Nag's Head is still there, very small and full of character, and The Wilton Arms, much larger and much loved. The Turk's Head is now a restaurant and bar offering 'an innovative cocktail list', 'a wonderful dining experience', 'a unique Sunday Roast experience' and a private room 'that can be tailored to your every requirement'. There is a Horse and Groom a few minutes' walk away but it's not the same one.

Dun Cows

The word 'dun' originally meant a dark, nut brown but has acquired, perhaps because of its sound, elements of dullness and dinginess, so that a lady describing her natural hair colour as mousey might also call it dun. As the Bard of Avon wrote:

> 'My mistress' eyes are nothing like the sun;
> Coral is far more red than her lips' red:
> If snow be white, why then her breasts are dun;
> If hairs be wires, black wires grow on her head.'

Given that a number of pubs were originally farmhouses, it could be deduced that the sign of the Dun Cow was a literal translation of what came before. Well, it could be, and it might be in some cases, and it probably is with The Red Cow, The Spotted Cow, The Cow and Hen and so on, but there is a much more interesting story behind The Dun Cow.

A poem, *Gui de Warewic*, by an unknown Twelfth Century author, was the real start of it although the roots of the tale go back further. In the poem, this ordinary Guy, son of a steward in the service of the Earl of Warwick, fell in love with a high-born lady called Felice, daughter of the Earl, no less. To prove himself worthy of the beauteous maid, he had to go off and perform

Specimens of this insect-eating mammal, remarkable for the low development of its brain, are few on pub signs. Here we are at Lichfield's recently converted manor house – please note the high-class woodwork of the signpost – but we could also go to Lydney or Crawley. The Dog and Hedgehog is in Nuneaton.

Another interesting fact about the hedgehog is that when born its spines are white and soft, for which we must imagine Mrs Tiggy-Winkle was duly grateful. No pubs are named for her or her creator, Miss Potter, although there is The Winkle in Basingstoke, The Crab and Winkle in Peterborough and The Leek and Winkle in Brighton.

No Comment in London

'There may be differences of opinion, but we venture to assert that recent structural alterations at the Bull and Bush have somewhat marred rather than improved the old familiar landmark. No longer now do the great bay windows, with drawn red blinds after nightfall, suggest homely comfort to the wayfarers of North End, since a more commodious tavern has been deemed necessary to meet the requirements of the ever-growing 'dry' residential district of Golders Green.'

More London Inns and Taverns, Leopold Wagner, 1925

Now describing itself as 'Country pub and eating house', more change has occurred.

'The Bull & Bush on the outskirts of Hampstead is one of North London's famous landmark pubs dating back to 1721. The pub has been wonderfully restored to its former glory incorporating the values of traditional pub hospitality together with modern designs featuring stone fired ovens, log burning hearths, deep leather seating and spacious teak furniture.'

We can only speculate as to what Mr Wagner might have had to say about stone fired ovens.

various brave deeds in the manner of Hercules. He rescued a royal damsel, slew several dragons and a giant, went on the Crusades and, having become Sir Guy, married the lovely Felice.

Still, the adrenalin of adventure gripped him, so when he heard about the monstrous Dun Cow of Mitchell Fold in Shropshire, he had to go and see it off. This was a cow like no other cow. She was immense and had an inexhaustible supply of milk, but one old dame was greedy and, after filling a pail, tried to fill a sieve as well. This rather upset the right-thinking cow and, using her hooves the size of cartwheels and her horns the length of a bull elephant's tusks, she broke free of the fold and rampaged across Dunsmore Heath, laying waste to everything and everyone in her path, except Sir Guy of course, who slew her.

There is another legend of a dun cow helping Ninth Century monks to found the city of Durham but it is, frankly, quite unbelievable. So, let us have one final chorus, please, of the traditional song:

> There was Brown, upside down, mopping up the whisky off the floor.
> 'Booze, booze' the firemen cried, as they came knocking at the door.
> Don't let 'em in till it's all mopped up. Someone shouted 'McIntyre'.
> And we all got blue-blind paralytic drunk,
> When The Old Dun Cow caught fire.

Georges

There are approaching 500 pubs with George in their names, about 100 of them with Dragons. A few have numbers like IV and V, one has a Fox, one a Pilgrim, one a Lobster, two have Vultures, and one is named for Canning of that ilk and one for Eliot. The George Canning, billed as 'Bar and Brasserie', is in Camberwell and is not The George Canning of old, the one in Tulse Hill/ Brixton at the corner of Effra Road and Water Lane, but both were named for the Liverpool MP, foreign minister and, briefly, Prime Minister in the times of Georges III and IV.

The Brixton George Canning used to have a statue outside, which was given the name Diogenes after a landlord of the 1850s retrieved it from the street and had it put up in his courtyard, it having fallen off the back of a waggon. This George became The Hobgoblin in 2003, and The Hobgoblin became an

---

No Comment in London

'Chelsea has always acted up to its traditions for the promotion of good fellowship. To-day the eventide company of light-hearted men at the Six Bells, chiefly drawn from the local studios, would be hard to match elsewhere in London.'

More London Inns and Taverns, Leopold Wagner, 1925

For a while, The Six Bells kitchen was the home of a new chef called Marco Pierre White then, in 1984, such a significant year, it turned into the Henry J Bean's Bar and Grill, offering food and drink to make every American think he was at home, with 'an extensive array of spirits and cocktails, served with a flair unique to the Bean's brand'.

inter-species cross between a Thai restaurant and a Scottish theme pub called The Hootenanny in 2007. One correspondent describes it as having 'all you could ask from a pub – pool tables, live music and giant screens'.

One of the many plain Georges, on Haverstock Hill, in 1925 was 'somewhat modernised, still preserves much of its antiquated character, but is now wholly lacking the tea gardens formerly associated with it'. In more recent times it became The Rat and Parrot, only to be born again as The George.

Signs of Old Times: The King's Breeches

This city-centre pub is very popular with exiles from the old Iron Curtain countries, since it reminds them so much of the railway station buffet bars back home. Connoisseurs of 1950s minimalism will also enjoy the five well-seasoned South American banknotes pinned to the stone-effect wallpaper above the bar.

Other establishments near-by offer a full menu plus blackboard specials, and live music in the evenings. The King's Breeches provides for a niche market to one side of the business-lunch crowd, with a small selection of superheated pies out of a Perspex cabinet. The free paper serviette assists easy eating rather than forcing on customers the embarrassing refinements of cutlery and plate. After dark, a jukebox can be switched on by special request and any record played, provided it is *Crystal Chandeliers*.

Lecturers from the art college, attracted by the working-class atmosphere, drink no more than two units while chattering incessantly and waving their hands about. Journalists and flat-capped regulars prefer to ensure inner cleanliness with sequential pints of the memorable local bitter, reading their sporting papers in silence, dreaming of the days when they could flick fag-ash into dampening lagoons on the mahogany tops of varnish-free Victorian tables.

The tenant landlord, a small, thin, dark, taciturn man who is never rude to anyone but never friendly either, is greatly distressing the brewery by not dying. The predictions of the Chief Actuary of the Publicans, Sinners and General Insurance Co. indicate that pub landlords' short-livedness is second only to those who combine Sumo wrestling with cave diving, but our man is past 70 and showing no signs. When he does die, the brewery will rip the pub asunder, put a manager in, rename it The Tup and Tart and give new impetus to the disk jockey, amplifier and herbaceous-substance industries.

One of the more famous Georges is the Inn at Wanstead, originally a George and Dragon and a coaching inn on route from London to Epping. The current Wanstead George, a massive London corner house built in 1904 and now run by Wetherspoon, still retains some of that old world charm despite numerous renovations.

Set into a wall is a plaque, from a previous incarnation dated 1752, restored in 1858 and rescued in 1904. It says: In Memory of Ye Cherry Pey As cost 1/2 a Guiney Ye 17 of July That day we had good cheer and hope to so do maney a Year. R C 1752 Dad Jerry.

The story goes that a group of builders were working on the frontage of the pub, using scaffolding. While sloshing lime mortar about and whistling at the local Hogarthian trollops, they hatched a plan to sequester a large pie they had seen being taken into the baker's shop next door for cooking. When it came out,

In Frodsham, Cheshire, there is a very busy spot with a rapid turnover in large numbers of real ales, which is the only pub in Britain called **The Helter Skelter**. It used to be The Gaping Gander, another unique name although there are two Gaping Gooses, both in the Leeds/ Bradford area. The Frodsham ex-Gander is named for the helter skelter at the fairground on Frodsham Hill, 'a lighthouse shaped structure down the outside of which pleasure-seekers slide seated on a

mat', says the *Shorter Oxford Dictionary*. Such structures are not thrilling enough for modern pleasure-seekers and helter skelters are not seen so often now.

The expression is much older than the structure. Shakespeare used it, and Ben Jonson. It's a rhyming figure like harum-scarum or pell-mell, the skelter bit being from an old English word for hurry up. The one who thus named the pub might have hesitated, had he consulted the aforementioned dictionary, where helter-skelter is given as 'characterised by disorderly haste or headlong confusion'. As a several-times customer at the pub, this writer can say that pleasure seeking was not so characterised.

borne high on a wooden tray, they swooped from their position of advantage and lifted the pie, which turned out to be cherry. Although they enjoyed the pie very much, an old spoilsport of a Rector had them arraigned before the Justice of the Peace, a man who happened to be keen to stamp out this sort of thing. Not being able to identify any single pie-snatcher, he collectively fined them half a guinea which, based on a building worker's wages in those days, would have been the equivalent of £750 modern money. They all chipped in. They'd had a good laugh, so one of the more skilled among them commemorated the event in stone, in special builders' spelling.

Some very boring people say this story isn't true and the plaque is nothing more than a simple celebration of a feast at the inn which happened to feature a giant cherry pie. The flimsy evidence for this is: (a) the landlord's name in 1752, David Jersey, which could have become Dad Jerry due to weathering and recarving; (b) that Wanstead was known for cherry orchards at the time; and (c) that enormous pies were often baked for festive occasions. Well, if you believe that, you'll believe anything.

Griffins

This Griffin, one of about 60 nationally, is in Fletching, Sussex, where it once rained soot. 'Upon June 22, 1884, at Fletching, Sussex there was intense darkness and that rain then brought down flakes of soot in such abundance that it seemed to be snowing black.' Regardless of colour and frequency of atmospheric precipitation, there are Griffins throughout the country, largely because the beast was very popular among the shield-bearing classes, symbolising as it did a lion and an eagle at the same time.

Your actual griffin was not, as heraldry portrays it, half of one and half of the other. Although it did resemble a blend of those two creatures, it was an animal in its own right, having a raptor's beak and wings and a muscular four-legged body, sometimes with a lion-like tail, sometimes with a serpent instead.

Of course, we all know now that there is no such thing as a griffin, but it was not always so. Greeks, Syrians, Romans and others believed it to live in Scythia, an outlandish area north of the Black Sea corresponding roughly to modern Ukraine, Georgia and Azerbaijan, where gold and jewels could be freely gathered like crab apples in autumn. Any strangers coming along with buckets and sacks were leaped upon by griffins and torn to shreds for their avarice.

In the civilised world, as opposed to Scythia, slightly more disciplined specimens were said to watch over gold mines, rather as Rhodesian Ridgebacks do today, and a team of especially gifted griffins drew the chariot of the Sun.

There is a Gryphon pub, in Grange Park, London, said to be named for the griffin-like creature ordered by the Queen of Hearts to take Alice to meet the Mock Turtle, but it could also be named for the small, conical, mud-spitting volcano called a gryphon. In any case, it's now a Harvester.

Kentish, or of Kent

A Man of Kent is one born east of the Medway, and a Kentish Man is one born to the west. Quite what that has to do with anything, we don't know, but The Kentish Drovers is on Peckham High Street, which is just off the Old Kent Road so that's understandable at any rate. The Kentish Quarryman is in Ditton, near Maidstone, an old working men's club converted to a pub proper in a village where once there was a stone quarry and now there is a nature reserve, and where they hold the world custard-pie throwing championships, if that makes any more sense than we've had so far.

There is a Kentish Yeoman in Seal, near Sevenoaks, and another one at Bearstead, Maidstone but, strangely, considering that the white stallion, the Kentish horse, is the county symbol, only one pub called The Kentish Horse, at Mark Beech, near Edenbridge. Quite what's happening in Dunks Green with The Kentish Rifleman on his sign, it's hard to tell. He is meant to be Home Guard; let's be glad the Germans didn't invade while he was filling his pipe.

There's a Kent Cricketers, several Duchesses of Kent mostly not in Kent, several Dukes, and ten Man of Kents but no Kentish Man. The Flower of Kent is in New Cross, which used to be Kent, and The Pride of Kent is in Staplehurst, which still is.

Kings', or King's, or Kings Heads, and Arms

There are about 300 pubs with the head of a king as their name and sign. Some of the very oldest ones would have been Pope's Heads before that, changing allegiance with Henry VIII's Reformation. Only slightly fewer, about 250, are King's Arms, presumably the arms of a single king rather than a guild or society thereof, a mere half dozen or so are plain Kings, and then we have specific kings such as Alfred, Arthur, Billy, Canute, both Charleses, Edwards, Georges, Harold, Henrys IV, V, VI and VIII, John, Williams – there are approximately 40 King William IVs – and even an Ethelbert in Reculver, and an Offa and an Oswy, plus the King ofs, such as Prussia or Diamonds, and a few King and, mostly Queens. If we say around 700 Kings altogether in various guises, we should be about right.

The King's Head, Laxfield, Suffolk, is universally known as The Low House because it's at the bottom of the hill on which the village is built and so was always the lowest, in terms of sea level rather than customers' morality, of the several pubs once thriving there. The king on the sign is indeed Henry VIII, a man who knew a lot about heads but is less frequently seen on pub signs than some other monarchs. That is not the only peculiar thing about The Low, in an age when so many publicans set out to attract crowds of foul-mouthed young men and women, the latter keen in their apparel to advertise their preparedness for sexual intercourse, the former expecting to take advantage after drinking twenty pints of lager but before, hopefully, having to throw up.

The Low is one of the very few pubs left in Britain that has no bar counter. You go in the taproom at the back, survey the array of barrels, and request whatever takes your fancy, which is drawn straight from the barrel in the non-headed manner preferred in those districts.

Before you reach the barrels, you pass through a room dominated by an ancient

Pub Rubbish Korner

'A particularly pleasant hostelry bearing the sign of the Sun in the Sands, in Shooter's Hill Road, was often made the objective of a Sunday stroll across the Heath by William Hazlitt and Leigh Hunt for the sake of the fine prospect of surrounding country from its open balcony. Shooter's Hill, by the way, never had the remotest connection with sportsmen, but was anciently dubbed 'Suitor's Hill' in popular derision of place-hunters proceeding along it in quest of backstairs influence when the Sovereign of these realms resided at Greenwich palace.'

Authority No 1

'Kentish drovers used to pass this way on their journey to the London market. When they climbed Shooter's Hill, having taken a week to get that far, and saw the setting sun through a cloud of dust and sand thrown up by the hooves of the sheep, they knew they were near the end of their journey.'

Authority No 2

'The first mention of a pub on this site is in 1790 with the name Sun Alehouse, though there is evidence that a building existed on the site in 1745 and it is likely it was a pub at that time. The building has been much altered over the years and there is a difference of thought as to if the pub was entirely rebuilt in 1842 or if it retains some of the original Eighteenth Century structure. The name developed into its current form due to the sandpits in the area.'

Authority No 3

'The interesting name is derived from the original Ye Sunne pub that would be lost in a cloud of dust as the local farmers drove their animals down the dirt tracks to Blackheath. The current pub dates from 1841 and these days it is more likely to be lost in the smog of car fumes from the A2. The interior is now one knocked-through cavernous room which makes it spacious but far too open.'

Authority No 4

For only three years and a bit, Anne Boleyn was Queen of England before having her head sliced off on trumped up charges, and her brother George too, and yet they named her local pub, the one at the gates of Hever Castle (the Boleyn family seat) after the man who ordered the slicing. Not only that but, while Anne long refused Henry's advances on the established principle of good salesmanship – that if you're told you can't have it you'll want it all the more – her elder sister Mary, also brought up at Hever, was rumpy-pumping away with the old carrot-top lecher. Mary lived to be 45 or thereabouts, which only goes to show something or other.

Mind you, Mary has no pubs named after her while dear Anne has two, The Anne Boleyn in Rochford and The Boleyn Tavern, Upton Park. The latter derives from the old name for West Ham United's football ground, the Boleyn Ground, which in turn comes from the club's purchase, in 1912, of the house and lands called Green Street House, aka Boleyn Castle because the Boleyns might have owned it.

To show that maybe there is some justice in the world after all, now that **The Henry VIII** in Skipton has been renamed The Snaygill Arms, Henry himself has only one pub fully named after him, and that's this one, and serve him right.

fireplace. Old settles, polished in parts by the backs and bottoms of the long dead, surround it in a U-shape, with a table in the middle. Another room, also called the taproom, has one large table and bench seats around. This is a social pub. If you want to be slightly less social you can go in the card room, which has small, separate tables and chairs, but otherwise you will be bound to get into conversation with people to whom you may not have been introduced.

There is no pool table, no piped music, no coin-in-the-slot of any kind, no television large or small. Dogs are welcomed and given a biscuit. The building is thatched, not so uncommon in Suffolk, and is obviously of considerable age. The other old pub still extant in the village, The Royal Oak, used to have settles in the same manner but a modernising landlord ripped them out some years ago. Their loss cannot be rectified.

Here is a report from the *East Anglian Daily Times*, occasioned by the sale of The King's Head to its then tenants in 1987:

'Time has almost stood still at the King's Head at Laxfield, which was 'saved' 15 years ago from the threat of so-called improvements when it was purchased by a local magistrate.

Beer is still drawn straight from the barrel in a back kitchen and the pub has been untouched by the successive booms in jukeboxes, 'fruit' machines and 'space invader' games.

No carpets adorn the brick, tile and stone floors and customers sit on hard benches and a few wooden chairs.

Now the pub is being sold once more, but there is no foreseeable threat to its simple splendour in a county where plastic beams, gassy beer, soft furnishings and piped music have become the norm … the normal means of socialising is through the almost forgotten art of conversation, customers sitting on a settle round an open fireplace and banging their mugs on the table when refills are required.' April 1987.

No word of that report needs altering today, except that banging mugs on the table is only done from time to time and that as a rather dangerous joke on the landlord, as we write, a burly fellow late of the Flying Squad.

Here is another report from the *EADT*, 1991:

'The previous landlords left large debts when they departed last year … bailiffs arrived and removed the ancient settles and other furniture which had helped make the pub so special. (The new tenants) went to the auction and bought them back but now say they cannot keep putting their money into the premises.'

The King's Head Inn, Chigwell, in 1918 looked about as olde worlde as you could possibly get. Now, as Ye Olde King's Head, it's more modern.

It is probably not one of the very oldest to carry that name, having Charles II as its emblem, although that in itself is not conclusive evidence as new signs for old pubs might pay respects to new kings. Some of the really old ones, pre-Reformation, could well have been Pope's Heads to start with. For the full story on kings' heads and other vital parts, see page 90.

Who's behind the bar?

'Possibly the first requirement in a barmaid or barman is that she/he should enjoy her/his work. An equable temperament is basic to the task. Too much hearty laughter can be as badly out of place as a morose countenance, and a skilful operator will judge and adjust himself to the mood of his customers, conversing with the talkative and respecting the privacy of the introspective.'

The Traditional English Pub, Ben Davis

The **Kirkstile Inn** at Loweswater, one of the smaller lakes by Buttermere and Crummock Water, was brewing its own beer at the time of writing although moving production to Hawkshead. This ancient hostelry is right by the church as you might expect and has been welcoming travellers allegedly since Tudor times. It's very much bigger than the hamlet of Loweswater might demand but needs to be, to cope with the throngs of ramblers who can hardly wait to skip up one of the smallish mountains round about so they can skip down again to a pint and a pie.

And so it closed, not for the first time but, we all hope, for the last, to reopen a few months later. In the New Year of 1994 it came to national attention when *The Times*, no less, reported thus:

'Rustic revelries were cut short on New Year's Day at the King's Head, a 14th century pub in Laxfield, Suffolk. The police arrived after fielding complaints over the noise created by four troupes of Morris dancers. Too many jingle bells, apparently.'

Quite where *The Times* got Fourteenth Century from, we cannot tell. It is a very old building but from the 1500s, that is the Sixteenth Century, according

As recently as 1993 **The Labour in Vain** in Yarnfield, Staffordshire, was showing its very incorrect sign, until a complaint was made about it. The village was split 50:50 on the matter but the owners, then Bass, took it down and replaced it with a sign saying Temporary Sign. New owners Enterprise, after a campaign for its restoration, allowed the sign to be preserved round the back as a curiosity, provided it could not be seen from the public highway.

There is an equally incorrect story from less sensitive days by Enid Blyton, in which a poor golliwog gets the tub treatment, but the idea is much older. The pub of the same name at Telford had a very similar sign, as did the one at Stourbridge but with two ladies ready to do the business, but that dated from before 1920. Maybe Ms Blyton got her idea from there; she couldn't have had it from The Labour in Vain, Douglas, Isle of Man, which had the same sign but had been knocked down by 1876.

There used to be another one at Billinge, near St Helens, but that's been demolished, and there's a Labour In Vain Yard in Norwich, an ex alehouse called Labour in Vain Cottage in St Ives – so we can see we've lost at least as many as we still have.

There are various ideas on how the name came about. Some say that it was a proclamation from the landlord, that any attempt to find a better pub with better beer would be a fruitless exercise. Similarly pointless would be any woman trying to pretend that certain matters were not the case, despite everybody in the village knowing all the details. It might also be a sly crack at those religious puritan types who fulminated against the evils of drink. Psalm 127 says 'Except the Lord build the house, they labour in vain that build it', so perhaps someone is saying 'Oh yeah?'

Here in Yarnfield, the birds now remind the ploughman how much they are looking forward to the day when he'll be sowing all that delicious wild bird food.

> They spoke of progress spiring round,
> Of Light and Mrs Humphry Ward –
> It is not true to say I frowned,
> Or ran about the room and roared:
> I might have simply sat and snored –
> I rose politely in the club
> And said 'I feel a little bored;
> Will someone take me to a pub?'
>
> *A Ballade of an Anti-Puritan*, G K Chesterton, 1874–1936

to the listing authorities. It was not originally an alehouse, we can be fairly sure of that, since the only purpose-built pubs from that time were inns on busy waysides and such could not be the case here. Henry VIII is on the sign, which might suggest a date but Henry is certainly an afterthought. According to report, at one time the sign had Henry VIII on one side and Charles I on the other.

It was an alehouse by the early 1700s, possibly before but we cannot tell. In 1855 it was one of five in the village, the others being The General Wolfe, The White Horse, Mrs Ann Chaston's unnamed house, and The Royal Oak which is still there. This was for a population of not quite twelve hundred.

The bar areas of The King's Head have been largely unaltered since Victorian times and the furniture dates from then or before, made in the farmhouse-joinery tradition. From the 1850s the pub was owned by Etheridge's Brewery of Eye, which became Fisher's Brewery in 1874. Adnams, then one of almost 10,000 independent brewers in Britain, bought it in 1904 and closed it in 1969. They sold it to that magistrate, a local farmer, in 1972 for £9,000. It went through several ownerships and some very difficult times, and Adnams, by then one of only 50 independent brewers in Britain, bought it again in 2001 for an undisclosed sum thought to be not un-adjacent to a lot.

The King's Head at Crouch End, north London, used to be known more familiarly as The Old Yard of Pork. The story, if true, is typical of what happens in pubs, where a great deal of what East Anglians call 'squit' is talked and acted upon. One day, an argument arose in the pub, the basis of it being that nobody ever bought pork by the yard. On the contrary, said one, he had often bought a yard of pork. He disappeared for a few moments, during which he visited the nearest butcher's shop, and came back into the bar with three feet, pig's feet you see, which were kept on display for some considerable time.

Lions, various

> 'So, seeking for further amusement,
> They paid and went into the Zoo,
> Where they'd Lions and Tigers and Camels,
> And old ale and sandwiches too.'

Marriott Edgar's lines are on Blackpool Zoo, in The Lion and Albert. They still have lions, tigers and camels there, and sandwiches in the licensed café, but not old ale we can be fairly sure. At the time of writing, such a beverage would not be offered in The Elusive Camel either, it being a trendy 'drinks bar' in London Victoria rather than a pub as such, although they might have it in The Camel in Bethnal Green. There is also The Camel and Artichoke in London Waterloo, and The Camel's Hump in Middlesbrough, but old ale – like common sense – isn't as common as it used to be.

As for tigers, there are about 30 if you include the Tiger Moths and the Tiger's Heads, far more than camels anyway. Tiger's Heads may be heraldic in origin; Sir Francis Walsingham, Queen Elizabeth I's right-hand man, had a tiger on his coat of arms, and there was always good reason to keep in with such a powerful chap.

And so we come to lions, of which there are more than 60 plain and many more in black, white, gold and so on. Most of these have heraldic origins. You might expect royal arms to figure strongly, but there are very few Lion and Unicorns (Stuart kings and William of Orange as well as our present monarch) – one in Stirling, one in Liverpool, one in Kentish Town – and only one Lion and Dragon, by the River Trent at Sawley, Notts, representing the last three Tudors, Henry VIII, Edward VI and Elizabeth I.

There are more than 70 Black Lions, including the one at Walsingham, pilgrimage town of north Norfolk, which house is said to have been partly built especially for a king, Edward III, to stay in when he came to the shrine. The name and sign are from the coat of arms of Edward's queen, Phillipa of Hainault, taken when the house became an inn in the 1500s. This king ruled for 50 years from 1327, married the 15-year-old Phillipa in 1328 at York Minster, and had fourteen children with her, including the Black Prince (eight pubs), and John of Gaunt who has five with his name and another 650 or so announced by his red lion.

> 'A glass device, suspended at right angles over the entrance to a truly captivating resort, and illuminated after dusk, arrests public attention in these terms: Black Lion Hotel. The Modern Tavern. Visit the new Balcony Lounge for Music and Entertainment with your Refreshment.

Three years ago this annexe of the Black Lion was a billiard hall, a felicitous conversion of the pioneer music hall, open only on Mondays and Saturdays, in the district. Though devoid of a circle and gallery, the place betrayed its former usage by the retention of the stage proscenium and drop curtain. All that has now changed. Beneath a comfortable balcony lounge with ferns and pot plants, facing the bar, is a series of cosy alcoves, each electrically lighted and, like the overhead lounge, having a staff of waiters in attendance, where the denizens of East Ham, both Man and Womankind, can spend the leisure hour while listening to good music in the true Continental style. Added to these attractions – factors of pure delight – the Licensing Justices have gone

---

Signs of Old Times: *Ye Olde Sunne Dryed Tomatoe*

Visitors to this remote and historic ex-hostelry, far up in the hills where rivers rise, always used to enjoy looking at the old photographs on the wall. These reflected a bygone age when the pub was The Drovers' Dog, the annual produce show was held here, the hunt met on Boxing Day, customers formed football, cricket and darts teams and there were Toyota pick-ups in the car park.

Yes, those were the days, my friends, when the pub was the social sine qua non of a scattered rural community. The community is still scattered but if anybody wants a pint now it has to be a widget tin from the supermarket down the valley, because pints have not been sold at Ye Olde Sunne Dryed Tomatoe for a twelvemonth.

Yes, in that short time Signor Pomodoro Lambretta, front of house, and Darren 'Sharon' McBarren, chef, transformed the place. Before, you could only get bitter, lager, Guinness and two sorts of sandwich: cheese and pickle, or cheese.

Under Pommy and Sharon, you could have Saltimbocca Siciliano, Fegato alla Milanese, Pavarotti alla Mariolanza and various fusion dishes, including Szechuan Ostrich Stroganoff and Thai Broken Harbour Soup with Wild Orkney Octopus. You washed these down with 35 different sorts of Bardolino and 27 of Frascati. If you got too merry you could have bed and full Italian breakfast for the price of a farm labourer's week's wages.

It was not long before the two proprietors discovered that Upper Weirdale was no place for a gastro-pub. Their loan was called in and they had to sell the place as a private house, so that was it.

the length of sanctioning the provision of a dance floor! Could anything better bespeak a fine discernment of public needs? Verily, what has been accomplished at The Modern Tavern in East Ham is worthy of emulation wheresoever local bodies have the moral and social improvement of the people in their hands.'

Leopold Wagner, writing in 1925 in his book *More London Inns and Taverns*, was a staunch supporter of the pub as venue for conversation, and not a man who embraced change eagerly. We can only imagine the scalpel-sharp satire he might have employed had he been able to see the moral and social improvements now being made to West Ham supporters on match days, and

There's a Jersey Lily in Bristol, but the most popular spelling is Lillie, as in **The Lillie Langtrys** in London, Norwich and elsewhere. This Langtry is in Stone, Staffordshire, with a sign exemplifying her legendary beauty.

Lillie Langtry was born Emilie Charlotte Le Breton in 1853. She became a famous actress and socialite, friend of Oscar Wilde – who wrote *Lady Windermere's Fan* for her and whose flatmate Frank Miles painted her dozens of times – as well as mistress of the great and the good. That she could pull is not in doubt. Her lovers included the Prince of Wales (generically about 200 pubs), the Earl of Shrewsbury (five pubs) and Prince Louis of Battenberg (no pubs). Louis was father of Earl Mountbatten, Viceroy of India et cetera; although no pubs were specifically named after him there are two called The Mountbatten.

Whatever happened to Lakeman's of Brixham?

In the middle of the Nineteenth Century there were something like 16,000 brewing companies and a similar number of pubs brewing their own beer. This amazing variety would only have been apparent to the traveller, of course. Most people lived their lives in the same place and drank whatever it was they had there.

Several of the 16,000 companies and brewing pubs were in the Devon fishing port of Brixham, population around 7,000 at the time, of whom 1,000 were in the fishing trade. In the brewing trade were the Lakemans, and had been since 1780. Family interest in the company ceased in 1901 but the name was kept, and by the 1930s the estate included 50 tied houses (Brixham now has less than half that number), and the competition from Bartletts and others was gone.

There were now less than 1,000 brewing companies in the UK, a dramatic reduction mostly due to the activities of firms like H & G Simonds of Reading, which had already bought breweries and estates in Devonport, Newbury, Wandsworth, Staines, Bristol and elsewhere. In 1937 it bought Lakeman's, and in 1950 closed the Brixham brewery.

By 1955, Simonds had 1,500 pubs, a big fish in a big pond that had eaten a great many little fish. Ah but, swimming alongside in 1960 came Courage, which had eaten Barclay and now ate Simonds. John Smith and other fish followed, then Courage itself was swallowed, regurgitated, swallowed again, and eventually ended up mating with Scottish and Newcastle. The offspring was called Scottish Courage. By this time, every trace of Lakeman, Simonds and Barclay, not to forget Stiles's of Bridgend, Bowly's of Swindon and May's of Basingstoke, and all the rest except John Smith, had been washed away. Surely no trace now can be found in the latest swallowing, that of the Courage bit of Scottish Courage sold to Charles Wells, the Bedford outfit where Young's of Wandsworth's beers are brewed.

There can be no finer description of the rationale behind this marvellous development than that given by an official S&N spokesperson: 'These new arrangements are part of S&N's continuous strategy to find the right organisational and ownership solutions for our brand equities.'

So that's what happened to Lakeman's of Brixham. Now you know.

As can be imagined from its exterior, **The Magnesia Bank**, known as The Maggie, of North Shields, was built as a bank in the 1850s, one of the first joint stock banks in the north east. Lloyds took it over and closed it when Shields developed commercially in a different area. It became the Central Social Club, which closed in the 1980s, then a pub.

The magnesia part of the name comes from an old cobbled street leading down to the Tyne, as shown on the sign, called the Magnesia Stairs. These sets of stairs, peculiar to North Shields, were built around 1760 onwards. They led from the old, overcrowded town on the riverside to the new town on higher ground. This particular stair was called Magnesia possibly because of early port activity, when people did not distinguish between lime and magnesium salts, believing them to be the same thing until 1754 when proof of their true chemical nature was shown. Northern Northumberland was known for its lime production, often exported from small, near-by harbours such as Seahouses but North Shields, with its trade in coal, may have offered a grander scale of things for the lime exporter.

to others via the four TV screens and the jukebox (dance floor still available, apparently), in that same Black Lion now addressing itself as in Plaistow. Leopold would have approved, we can believe, of the small lounge bar without TV where he might have retreated for a pint of recognisable ale.

Golden Lions number over 100, usually with heraldic causes and there are many such. Royal coats of arms, and others of the leading old families such as the Percys of Northumberland, liked to have lions as symbols of their power and bravery. There are even more White Lions, 160 or so, which is a little odd as almost every colour of lion outnumbers the white in heraldry. The only king to emblazon the white lion was the Yorkist Edward IV, an affable, charming sort of chap who, beneath the pleasantries, was as much a tyrant as any of them, if not more so. Idle and much given to wine, women and song, one might imagine a few pubs with his name as well as his lion, but no. There's a good dozen of Edward VIIIs but no Edward IV. Similarly, there's a good dozen of blue lions but only one Green Lion, on the A2 at Rainham in Kent.

Puddings, various

According to one source it was privately nicknamed The Butcher's after certain rather violent incidents took place there, but The Old Two Puddings, Stratford Broadway, east London, was much frequented by celebrities of all types in recent times. Pop stars, footballers and racketeers mixed freely with hit men, second-hand car dealers, journalists and solicitors. The distaff side was as likely to be represented by gangsters' molls as fashion models and housewives. It was indeed a place where citizens met as equals at the bar but we can guess hardly any of them knew why the place was called The Old Two Puddings, or that there are two quite different versions of the story.

One authority states with complete conviction that a licensee of the pub, then called The Wheatsheaf, used to distribute pieces of plum pudding to the poor and needy at Christmas. Two enormous puddings were made and the landlord would stand between them, dishing out the slices.

Another authority, with equal conviction, states that the aforesaid Wheatsheaf was noted for the excellence of its steak, kidney and mushroom puddings which were served at any time this roadside house was open. Two wise men, hastening from the east into London town one evening, decided to stop at this hostelry to sample the famous puddings of which they had heard great things. The landlord, much to his own surprise, discovered on request that, business having been exceptionally brisk that day, there were only two puddings left. He hadn't eaten since breakfast and had promised himself a pudding, so he declared that he would have one and the two customers would have to share the other.

The customers said that this was inconsiderate, inhospitable and unreasonable, the customer is always right and so forth, but the landlord would not be moved, demonstrating his resolution by starting on the one pudding and threatening to eat the other as well if they didn't stop arguing. Consoling themselves with the thought of their scheduled dinner later, at Simpson's in the Strand, the two travellers conceded defeat with half a pudding each.

Which of these stories is true we cannot know, nor even if either is true. What we can say is that The Old Two Puddings, at the time of writing, is renamed as The Latin 1/4.

The Pudding and Pye, Wimborne is a big old pub in the centre of town, and The Plum Pudding, on the canal near Rugely, is operated mainly as a restaurant. And that's it for puddings. Only two left.

White horses, and horses of a different colour

The earliest known use of the white horse as a sign is in the 1400s but it could go back further than that through its widespread use in heraldry, by royal families from the kings of Wessex to the Hanoverians, by the London Guilds and by all sorts of local families.

The result is well over 300 pubs and hotels called The White Horse. They're everywhere. There's even the White Horse Triangle in Suffolk, its sides only four or five miles long with White Horses at the three points of Badingham, Rendham and Sibton Green. The latter is a tiny village less than a mile from the much larger Peasenhall, where there are shops, a café and a pea festival, but The Swan, The Angel and The New Inn are all closed. In case we were missing the point, there is also the defunct White Horse, closed about ten years ago, less than a mile from Rendham, and another in business in Framlingham.

Badingham White Horse.

The White Horse that was, at Sweffling.

Bay Horses are not far short of the hundred mark but quite why there should be so many is not clear, unless it is simply a measure of that type of horse's popularity and widespread success at the races. A proper bay horse, as eny fule kno, is a chestnut with black tail, mane

Rendham White Horse.

and ear edgings, the chestnut colour being anything from a light copper to a deep mahogany or darker.

Black Horses are more numerous than Bays, not far short of the white version, in the order of 250. We have two Blue Horses, four Brown Horses, three Chestnuts, and half a dozen Cock Horses. A cock horse was originally a hobbyhorse or anything a child did its pretend riding on, such as a broomstick. Later, the term came to mean a high horse or a big stallion for the hunt. The Cock Horse in Tonbridge has a sign showing a large white draught horse leading a team of brown ones at the plough, which is quite, quite wrong.

We also have Dark Horses, Dun Horses, quite a lot of Flying Horses, many Pack Horses, and Grey Horses as noted elsewhere. There are Racehorses,

Pub Rubbish Korner

Opposite each other on Headingley Lane, at the top of St Michael's Lane, Leeds, stand two pubs, The Original Oak and The Skyrack. They have both been rather overwhelmed by the massive student population up that way and have been gutted to cope with numbers that could not be fitted into their old arrangements. As late as 1967, the many-roomed and much-panelled Oak had a Gentlemen Only bar. Before that, the Skyrack was a quiet, wayside Dutton's house.

Howsomever, their names have an ancient significance. You may see all sorts of explanations about Sky and Rack, including one about a rack of clouds in the sky, but that is rubbish and nothing whatever to do with it.

Skyrack is not sky-rack, but skyr-ack or, more properly, *scir ac*, from the Anglo-Saxon verb *sciran*, to determine, and *ac*, oak tree, which is the way they still say it in Cumbria. Beneath the oak was where the council of elders met, to debate and decide upon disputed matters and, roughly where the war memorial now presides, is where that oak grew.

So, you see, both pubs really have the same name, one in modern English and one in the old language.

Running Horses, and Seahorses, which should really be classified with The Cod and Lobster in Staithes.

Of the Horse ands, Groom is the most popular adjunct with Jockey second, plus a few Trumpets and Ploughs. There are also the and Horses, including Coach (lots, over 100) Waggon (getting on for 100) Boat and Cart; and all the Horseshoes (200 or so of them) in fours, singles and the plain plural, and threes – which is usually said to imply a horse losing a shoe, and a blacksmith's shop next door to the pub. That blacksmiths often

The White Horse at Sibton Green.

Pub Rubbish Korner

'The one historic inn anywhere round London upon which the despoiling hand of the builder has never been at work is assuredly the Spaniards … whitewashed brick walls and green-shuttered windows with small glass panes striking a note of simplicity. Wainscoted walls, tiled floors and rude forms and tables characterise the bar and smoking parlour. Enclosed in a small show-case over the serving counter are three curious knives and forks with bent handles which were actually being used at supper by Dick Turpin and two trusted associates when word reached them that King George's men were in sight.'

More London Inns and Taverns, Leopold Wagner, 1925

'The Spaniards Inn has been a boozer since 1580.'

Time Out magazine

There are two main reasons offered for why this pub is called The Spaniards. One is that it was built around 1585 as the residence of the Spanish ambassador; the other that the old house was bought by two Spanish brothers in the mid 1700s who turned it into an inn on the increasingly busy country lane that it sat on. In any case, Dick Turpin was dead and gone many years before it had its licence.

took up such a position cannot be disputed, there being good business from the coaches, and from the farmers and carters who might like a pint while Dobbin was being shod. Even so, The Three Horseshoes is heraldic, and is on the coat of arms of the Farriers' Company.

There is also a Horsebreaker's Arms, near Thirsk, so called apparently because a landlord of old was known for his skills with uncouth equines.

Including all the other horse-related names that don't mention horse, such as Yorkshire Grey, Nag's Head, Old Grey Mare and so on, there must be approaching 2,000 pubs thus signified, which is on a par with crowns and kings. Perhaps this is as it should be although many would argue that a horse is rather more useful than a crown, or a king come to that.

There are two Copper Horses, one of which, in Seamer, North Yorks, used to be The White Horse. Your correspondent knows this because he had his 21st birthday party there. Soon after, a Scarborough bookmaker bought it and, to show he was a new broom, knocked the ancient pub all into one and renamed it after an odds-on favourite. He couldn't, of course, rename the street on the corner of which it stands, which is still White Horse Lane.

Curiously, although we are familiar with a man called Horse, we should seek in vain for a pub called it.

> 1st Murderer: Then stand with us.
> The west yet glimmers with some streaks of day;
> Now spurs the lated traveller apace
> To gain the timely inn, and near approaches
> The subject of our watch.
>
> *Macbeth*, III, William Shakespeare, 1564–1616

CHAPTER FIVE

Decline and Rebirth of an Industry

But to what have we given birth? John Mann, no relation to the brown ale, developed a special interest in the brewing industry during his many years studying the markets and government funding in the City of London. It's a long story, he says, and this is the short version:

No Comment in London

'Touching recherché saloons and alluring appointments generally, the Nelson Arms in Merton High Road is as enchanting a hostelry as anyone might wish to beguile away his time in. An exceedingly well-made encaustic tile representation of Nelson's flagship, the Victory, in full sail, adorns the entire side wall. Furthermore, it contains the nearest approximation to a 'smoke room' in the provincial sense that a licensed victualler all London round can boast of. The apartment actually so labelled is replete with green baize top tables, armchairs, ferns and box plants, pictures and illustrated periodicals, in short, everything conducive to suggest a superior club-house. As an object lesson of the way in which real public-house reform might be brought about without offending the susceptibilities of the licensing justices, the Nelson Arms at Merton would repay a whole day's journey to visit.'

More London Inns and Taverns, Leopold Wagner, 1925

'There are so many bad pubs in London and it's refreshing to drink in a place that gets everything right and where the owners actually care about more than just the bottom line.'

Mr Wagner's modern equivalent, a pub review on the internet, September 2009

'You turn a corner and find yourself gazing down a steep toboggan slope with gabled irregular houses bending over it on either side, making a scar of white on a green hillside. Almost at the top is the New Inn, which is incredibly old and as full of Americans as Stratford-upon-Avon. Its dining room is filled with old china, old oak, old brass, old everything that the ultra-modern could wish to buy. Models of a soldier and a sailor, swinging cricket bats as if they were Indian clubs, sway about in the wind above the inn. We walk into or stumble past postcard shops, tea-houses …'

S P B Mais, *Glorious Devon*, 1928.

Our photograph was taken in 1901 and the bat-swinging military men are already there, also the teahouses and postcard shops. Anyone who has been to Clovelly should be able to spot the deliberate mistake.

This **New Inn** is said to be Seventeenth Century and many of that name are from that time or earlier, almost by royal decree since Elizabeth I criticised the lack of suitable hostelries for the traveller. Otherwise the name may indicate a replacement inn on an old site. There are well over 200 New Inns, including Ye Olde New Inn (not

'Inne'?) at Arley in Worcestershire, which is about 300 yards from The New Inn, Bewdley, and 200 more are called The New something else – New Penny, New Broom, New Moon, New Recruit and so on.

The furore and disappointment which has greeted each of the recent spate of pub closures underlines the pub's importance to our way of life. But this same trend should remind us that pubs, their owners and suppliers are under constant financial and economic pressures. How have these pressures caused brewers, previously serving local needs, to become huge national businesses, only to disappear and be replaced by other businesses, which in turn, are now fighting for survival?

There are about 60 pubs named after the various Unities of Oddfellows; societies of support, charity and friendship with their origins in the old guilds of the City of London and not unlike the freemasons in possession of secrets, signs and rituals. Chief among them was the Manchester Unity; they and all the others used to meet in pubs. Modern Oddfellows, nationwide but sprung of Manchester with that name now dropped, have their own lodges.

This pub is in Chinley and depicts the fellows as odd in the sense of peculiar, although the first ones were odd in the sense of being left out of things by the snobby and wealthy guild masters, and needing to band together for mutual benefit. Their stratagem was not to insist on membership of a particular trade or craft. All were welcome to a general guild, so they were doubly odd, in being odds and sods as well as beyond the pale.

Breweries are large, capital intensive factories. To be economic, they need to work at high capacity but, through the first half of the Twentieth Century and beyond, peacetime beer consumption was on a downward trend. Over that time it fell by about a quarter, in a market that was restricted locally in size and competitiveness by our licensing system, which gave magistrates the power to decide if a licence to sell beer, wine and spirits should be granted, or not.

In response, some brewers merged and built up large chains of pubs to provide a secure market for their products. In general, it was brewing the beer that made the money, while the pub estate took care of itself. However, the ownership of a large property portfolio provided the security for the brewers to raise relatively large amounts of loan capital with which to finance the development of their businesses. By the 1960s, about three-quarters of pubs were occupied by a tenant through the tied-house system. The brewer would charge the tenant a nominal rent on the property and take a wholesale profit margin on the drink sold to him, which was known as 'wet rent'. Tenants especially resented the high prices they were charged for spirits while being

The **One Eyed Rat** in Ripon was previously The Lord Nelson, which at least explains the one eye and the nautical costume of the rodent in question. To get ratted, to be rat-arsed, to be in or see the rats, are all expressions closely associated with wholehearted consumption of the demon drink.

This pub, at the time of writing at any rate, is one espousing the virtues of proper beer, eschewing the common attractions of television, boy-racer music and food. There are, as far as we can tell, no other one-eyed rats in the country although there are plenty of Rat and Parrots, which seem to fulfil a need at the other end of the market place.

told what they could charge their customers, in the public bar at any rate. Older drinkers will remember when a Scotch cost rather more than a pint and people would ask a round buyer if he'd mind them having a short. Well, that was why. It was the brewers.

The larger brewers also stipulated the price of beer sold in the public bar, as an element in their competitive policies. Traditionally, most beer was drunk by working men, and working men went in the public. The brewers wanted to sell as much beer as possible therefore they squeezed the tenant on what he could charge. The tenant was allowed to charge a higher price in his lounge bar to an extent that his customers would accept.

The remaining pubs, the quarter not tenanted, were either free houses or run by a manager employed by a brewery. A noble exception to all these trends was Guinness, which didn't own any pubs and relied on generous wholesale and retail profit margins, backed by heavy marketing expenditure, on its distinctive brew.

Beer consumption revived in the 1960s as the post-war birth bulge reached drinking age, but other pressures emerged. Predators from outside the industry noticed the brewers' large property interests. These not only included pubs but also the brewery buildings themselves, which often occupied important city-centre sites. In 1959, with his eyes on the Stag Brewery in Victoria, London, Charles Clore bid for Watney's, but failed. In 1961 a Canadian entrepreneur, Eddie Taylor, spread panic through brewers' boardrooms as he built up a chain

Whatever happened to Becky's?

In London in the 1960s and early 1970s, as your correspondent was pleased to be, there was a truly remarkable institution called Becky's Dive Bar. It was in Southwark, just over the river, in a basement of a massive building, the Hop Exchange, although hops had not been exchanged there since 1920. Becky's was a very unusual pub. It defied most of the principles of pubness, in that it was furnished in the front parlour style out of the back street saleroom, it had appalling toilets, it wasn't clean and polished, and it was not so much decorated in the wrong colours as not really decorated at all. There was background music too, well, sometimes, and entirely at random, from an electro-mechanical instrument that many young people today will not have seen, a gramophone.

The pub was difficult to find, largely because enjoyment therein last time you were there had led you to forget its precise location. When you did find it, you went down some dark and precipitous stairs, not all of them entire, to be confronted by the aforementioned saleroom sofas and armchairs, and an array of barrels. This was unique in London at that time, because the barrels contained a changing range of beers from foreign parts of England, such as north of Watford. Becky also stocked a seemingly unlimited array of bottles of what you might call world beers, but we went for the draught Thwaite's and the Ruddle's.

The barman, Harry, claimed to be able to organise beer on request, from anywhere in Britain, so you'd say, what about Cameron's Strongarm? And he'd say, it's coming in next week. Barnsley Bitter? Next week. Chester's Fighting Mild? We've ordered it. Should be in next week.

Of course, when you went next week it was still Thwaites and Ruddle's but we didn't mind. You couldn't get them, or the other beers that popped up from time to time, anywhere else in the great ocean of Courage, Charrington and Watney that we otherwise navigated.

Mrs Becky Willeter closed her dive bar in 1975, that she'd opened as a sandwich shop in 1954, and that was the end of that.

of small breweries to form United Breweries. (This subsequently merged with Charrington, which then merged with Bass.)

Thus was provoked another wave of defensive mergers through which regional brewers reorganised into national groups. For example, in 1961

Allied Breweries was formed by the merger of Tetley in the north, Ansell's in the midlands, and Ind Coope in the south. By the end of the decade, seven companies were producing about three-quarters of the total UK output: Allied Breweries, Bass Charrington, Courage Barclay, Guinness, Scottish & Newcastle, Watney Mann, and Whitbread. Many fine, local and distinctive beers disappeared. They were replaced with what the brewers wanted consumers to drink, rather than what the drinkers wanted.

In particular, the sixties saw the emergence of more profitable, pasteurised keg beers. These were backed by heavy marketing and were supposed to provide a consistent quality, a notorious failing of 'real' beer being that it could be very good but it could also be awful. Our living rooms were infiltrated with advertising refrains sung to manly marching tunes:

> What's the beer that men like best?
> Watney's Draught Red Barrel.
> The special brew that beats the rest,
> Watney's Draught Red Barrel.
> Drink Red Barrel near or far
> In pub or club or any bar.
> It's always good wherever you aaaaaaa-are,
> Trust Watney's Draught Red Barrel.

By 1970, sales of keg beer had increased from one per cent to 14 per cent of the total. It approximately took up the share of draught mild beer, which fell from 40 per cent of the market to 24 per cent, partly reflecting the decline of beer as a thirst quencher for those working in heavy industry.

Brewers were spending more money on their pubs. They were becoming places to take the missus out on an evening or, more probably, for a young hopeful to ply a new girlfriend with Babycham. In tandem with these trends, the number of pubs also started to recover. After hitting a low point of about 70,000 in 1960, there were about 90,000 in 1980.

The brewers had woken up to the value of their licensed estates as profit centres in their own right, to some extent prompted by government investigations into their industry. In 1968/69, the Monopolies Commission investigated the tied-house system. In a report entitled 'The Supply of Beer', it concluded that the tied-house system was against the public interest but it would be impracticable to dismantle. Instead, it proposed some relaxation of the licensing laws, which it hoped might stimulate competition.

Almost immediately afterwards the industry was investigated again, by the Prices and Income Board. The price of beer in the public bar was hot

The **Peveril of the Peak**, a Victorian pub in Manchester unaltered since before World War Two, has a story that goes back much further, to the Norman Conquest. One of the Conqueror's alleged sons, said to have been born on the wrong side of the blanket, was William Peveril and he was granted the Royal Manors of the Peak to maintain on the King's behalf. He built a castle there, in Castleton, called Castleton Castle. It was also known as Peveril Castle, which is just as well or Sir Walter Scott's longest novel (yes, there really is one longer than *The Antiquary*) would otherwise have had to be called Castleton of the Peak.

Anyway, when the novel became famous after its publication in 1823, the managers of a stagecoach company that had a service running between Manchester and London, named the said service after it. Although it is possible that the pub was named after the novel, it is generally accepted that it was named after the coach.

politics and a component of the Cost of Living Index. Thus, any attempt on the part of the brewers to raise this price put them in the firing line. This was especially true in the periods of Labour government as the brewing industry was a declared financial supporter of the Conservatives. In fact, the brewers were allowed small increases in prices to finance further investment in their estates. Ironically, some of this investment was used to absorb the public bar into the lounge, a process justified as a response to the changing profile of the consumer, and to the rising cost of wages. Cut the number of bars and you can usually cut the number of bar staff, meanwhile raising prices up to saloon bar levels rather than down to those in the public bar.

The other important outside influence was the introduction of drinking and driving legislation in October 1967. After an immediate blip downwards, the overall growth in beer consumption resumed, but the new law did have an influence on the location of demand. Prior to the introduction of the breathalyser, it had been a popular custom to drive out to country pubs for a drink. Very gradually, and in response to the increased rigour with which the police pursued drinking and driving, this practice withered. To combat the loss of wet trade, many country pubs in effect became restaurants. Many large roadside pubs didn't survive. Drinkers stayed in town.

The other resistance to the brewers' market power at around this time came from CAMRA, the Campaign for Real Ale. Founded in 1971 with the less snappy name of Campaign for the Revitalisation of Ale, this organisation attracted widespread sympathy and support and helped focus the minds of consumers and politicians on what was happening to the national pint. Rather like the little boy in the Danny Kaye song who could see that the king was in the altogether, CAMRA told the drinking world that keg beer wasn't very nice.

Sales started to wane. Some brewers responded by resurrecting regional brews. Whitbread put its muscle behind Boddington's, the cream of Manchester, the Watney group rediscovered Webster's of Halifax; Scottish & Newcastle started brewing Theakston's at its Carlisle brewery. CAMRA also ensured that the brewers remained in the public eye; official investigations into the industry have been a near permanent feature. It is a measure of CAMRA's success that in the twelve years after its foundation, 200 new breweries were started, of which 140 were still on the go at the end of that period. Even Marks & Spencer was selling bottled real ale. CAMRA now has 200 branches and over 100,000 members.

Generally, the brewers managed to parry or ride all the blows and the 1970s were marked by another surge in corporate activity, this time in more diverse areas. In 1969/70, Allied Breweries attempted to merge with the Anglo-Dutch soap-to-food group Unilever. This fell through so they bid for Trust House Forte, the hotel and catering group, two years later. This also failed, and the company's itch would not be finally scratched until the acquisition of J Lyons & Co in 1978. Members of the WI at Worlingham-on-the-Water held hopes that The Spotted Bull would now serve afternoon teas as in the old days; such hopes were to be

Older readers may remember jumping about to a rock band called the Piltdown Men. They were heavy on the saxophones while playing *Old Macdonald had a farm* and calling it *Macdonald's Cave*, and the *William Tell Overture* calling it *Piltdown Rides Again*. What sophisticates we were, in the days of *Six-Five Special*.

Anyway the famous **Piltdown Man** hoax, in which human skull fragments mixed with the jawbone of an orang-utan were 'accidentally' found and put forward as the missing link, was so

widely believed that they renamed the village pub after it in the 1920s. The hoaxers, who have not been securely identified, are thought to have set it up to make the principal in the matter, Sir Arthur Smith Woodward, look like an idiot. They must have been terribly disappointed when the world believed it all for so long, from 1912 really until the early 1950s. The usual suspect, Charles Dawson, died three years after the 'find'; so he'd be even more disappointed if it was him.

rekindled twelve years later with the acquisition of Dunkin' Do'nuts. Regulars at The Boilermakers' Arms in the Yorkshire mining village of Urdley were not alone in failing to see the industrial logic behind these moves.

Watney Mann finally succumbed to a bid from the hotel group Grand Metropolitan in 1972. In both Allied Lyons and Grand Met, brewing and pub owning interests were progressively marginalised and ultimately disposed of, and it was the same story for some of the other majors as the merry-go-round spun on into the 1980s. Imperial Tobacco bought Courage as part of an attempt to diversify from its declining tobacco interests, then Hanson Trust bought Imperial Tobacco, splitting up its constituent parts and selling Courage to Elders IXL, the Australian owner of Fosters, who had unsuccessfully tried to bid for Allied Breweries the year before. Elders then attempted to buy Scottish & Newcastle. The OFT referred this to the Mergers & Monopolies Commission. At the same time, possibly provoked by a spate of sharp beer price increases, 'The Supply of Beer' was again investigated. After two years' deliberation, the MMC produced its report in 1989.

He looks kind of cheerful but clearly aware of a hard day's work in front of him, when possibly he might rather be at school. His future, however, is not an academic one, nor will it be until mechanisation releases him to new opportunities.

There are four **Ploughboys**, at Saltash, Lincoln and Green Ore, Somerset, and this one on the original Roman route from Buxton to Manchester, at Disley.

Before pondering on this momentous event, it is important to have another look at what was happening in the market place. The gap in the market left by the demise of sweet and fizzy keg bitters was more than filled by the rapid growth in demand for lager. At the time of the Monopolies Commission report of 1969, draught lager formed barely one per cent of the beer market, which ten years later had become about 30 per cent and now is something like 60 per cent, outselling real ale by six pints to one. Lager's earliest foothold in the market was in Scotland, where it was often taken as a whisky chaser, but it also corresponded to beer sold abroad. Drinkers returning from their overseas holidays found its low temperature and bland sweetness both appealing and refreshing. Although British brewers enjoyed success with brews such as Carling and, for a while anyway, Harp and Skol, the new popularity of lager opened the market for international brewers and brands. Carlsberg, Stella Artois, Kronenberg and Heineken became the new market leaders.

Meanwhile, the pub was becoming more profitable. By the time of the second MMC report, retailing was matching brewing as a profit centre. This meant that pubs were capable of standing alone, which had not been the case back in 1969.

The report was released in March 1989. Its contents astonished the media and the brewers. It agreed with the earlier conclusion: that the tied-house system was against the public interest. Its main proposals, known as the Beer Orders, were that no brewer should own more than 2,000 pubs and that tenants should offer one guest beer. This meant that 22,000 pubs were to be put on to the market or released from the tie. Generally, the press supported the radical

No Comment in London

'The vast majority of Londoners associate Nunhead only with an immense cemetery and an aggregation of small dwellings. Little do they divine that the Old Nun's Head, facing the triangular patch of green, was for upwards of two hundred years the most noted pleasure haunt in the environs of South London. More extensive than those of the Peckham Bun-House or the Dulwich Green Man, its tea gardens belonged to a Nunnery suppressed at the Reformation. When the emissaries of the much-married monarch waited upon the Lady Superior with an order of expulsion, she offered such stout resistance that she was murdered, and her head left stuck on a pikestaff in the centre of the little green. Meanwhile the sisterhood took flight through a subterranean passage to an altogether unsuspected outlet behind the King's Arms in Meeting House Lane.'

If that's true, it must have been one wonderful subterranean passage. The above description was written in the 1920s. The next is from 1878.

'On the north-east side of Peckham Rye is Nunhead, which is rapidly becoming a place of some importance, with a large population, and the head quarters of various centres of industry.

Nunhead Green, an open space about one acre in extent, still remains; but its surroundings are now very different to what they were half a century ago, when village lads and lasses were wont to dance and romp there, and when the ancient 'Nun's Head', which has been an institution in the locality for above two hundred years, was an object of attraction, through its tea-gardens, to worn-out citizens.

Here is the Asylum of the Metropolitan Beer and Wine Trade Association, which dates from 1851, when, at a general meeting of the beer-trade as a protection society, the idea assumed a substantial form, and a subscription was opened. The beer-sellers actively bestirred themselves to imitate the good example set by the licensed victuallers, by seeking to provide an asylum for their aged and decayed members. It comprises seven houses, each containing four rooms and a kitchen, accommodating in all thirteen inmates, and a piece of garden-ground in the rear for the use of the inmates is attached to each holding. In 1872 a new wing was completed, by the erection of eight six-roomed houses, thus providing accommodation for sixteen more inmates. There is an allowance of 6s. per week to single inmates, and 9s. per week to married couples.'

Six shillings would have bought 30 or 40 pints of ale at The Old Nun's Head in 1878. Basing values on earnings, an allowance of six shillings would be something like £150 now, for which one could buy 30 or 40 pints of ale at The Old Nun's Head.

nature of these proposals but the brewers were up in arms, and what about the politicians?

During the course of the report's preparation there had been a change of government. Margaret Thatcher and the Tories had come to power and they faced a dilemma. This was a government that lived by its competition and free market policies, and the brewers were among its most ardent financial supporters. After due deliberation, the new government was 'minded to accept' the MMC proposals. There was fury among Tory back-benchers and a large revolt was threatened. In the July, a compromise version was proposed which halved the number of pubs to be disposed of, and confined the guest beer provisions to the national brewers. Even this left the brewers in a mess; they were selling unpopular products to a market they no longer owned.

Courage stopped retailing. Grand Met stopped brewing. Allied merged its brewing with Carlsberg. Bass sold some 400 pubs to the newly formed Enterprise Inns and later split the rest of the business in two, the pubs going under the Mitchells & Butlers brand. Nevertheless, by offering large bulk discounts, the national brewers succeeded in hanging on to market share for several years.

Very few of the pubs on sale went to their incumbent tenants as the MMC and the politicians had expected, partly because there was a property recession at the time. Instead, they went to specially formed large retail groupings. Some of these were rather distant from British brewing. For a while, the Japanese investment firm Nomura held the largest pub estate in the country. Locals at The Dog and Duck in Upper Waxingham were worried that their pub might become a sushi bar. The local dogs and ducks were worried too.

The main pub owners became Inntrepreneur, Pubmaster, Enterprise Inns and Punch Taverns. The common feature of these firms was their unusually heavy borrowing, secured on their property and serviced from their tenants' rents. This was fine in the buoyant decade that followed, and the financial press enthused. In addition, newer chains were formed such as J D Wetherspoon plc and Slug & Lettuce, which offered competitive prices in their pubs and often employed new locations. Old bank branches were deemed especially suitable. Even the pump room at Harrogate spa was not sacrosanct.

The European Commission had never liked the tied-house system, which required an exemption from EEC regulations. In 1995, it asked our Office of Fair Trading to investigate why brewery tenants had to pay higher wholesale prices for beer than the free trade and the pub chains. The OFT concluded that strong retail competition existed and bulk discounts were part of this. In other words, it approved the status quo. In 2002, the Beer Orders were revoked but the horse had long bolted. The major pub owners were now Enterprise Inns and Punch Taverns, with over 15,000 pubs between them.

Some of the smaller brewing groups, which had been exempt from the Beer Orders, were beginning to flex their muscles. In particular Greene King, the East Anglian brewer, raised its profile with a number of shrewd acquisitions. With its large free trade, the group is now virtually a national brewer. Fuller's of Chiswick have acquired Gale's, and Young's have merged their brewing interests with those of Charles Wells. In recent years, these groups have done well as the ambitions of the former majors have been redirected by their international owners.

Pubs commemorate getting on for 50 poachers, their pockets and their most famous exponent, from Lincolnshire, whose delight the trade was on a shiny night in the season of the year. This poacher, the only one with Arms, on the road from Hope to Castleton in the Peak District, is obviously an upmarket one, risking his neck for the king's deer.

The pub too has had a major refit to bring it up to the mark. An inn with no chimney pots around it has to attract custom from elsewhere.

Since 2007, the industry has been going through a period of crisis. As mentioned above, some of the new pub-owning groups were heavily indebted. In recent conditions, such loan facilities have proved difficult to renew. This is partly due to the problems within the financial sector and partly due to deteriorating trading conditions in the pub groups, which in turn are blamed on financial pressures on the consumer and the smoking ban, which was introduced in England in July 2007, a year earlier in Scotland. Perhaps even more important is the competition from supermarkets, which often use beers and lagers as loss-leaders, frequently at less than half the price a pub will charge.

Landlords complain but the government will always be more interested in the inflation figures than publicans' livelihood. Rural pubs have been especially badly affected, unless they work very hard on their dining facilities. Closures are no longer newsworthy and the For Sale signs probably understate the number of pubs on the market. One issue of the trade paper, *The Morning Advertiser*, at the time of writing was offering 2,997 pubs for sale, which was no more than that part of an iceberg visible above the waterline.

An announcement is awaited on whether the OFT should investigate 'The Supply of Beer' once again with special reference to the requirement of tenants to buy beer from their landlords. Given the precarious nature of the latter's finances this will be a delicate judgement. The record of official meddling, however well meaning, is not encouraging.

CHAPTER SIX

Two Brewers

After selling his international marketing consultancy, Interbrand, John Murphy decided to try his hand at being a brewer. Rather than follow what might be called the conventional route – setting up a microbrewery to supply a small number of pubs with characterful draught beers named after the private parts of domestic animals – he decided to do something different. Here are his thoughts on the matter, and on why he doesn't own an estate of pubs to go with his brewery.

Holland has Heineken, Germany has Becks, the USA has Budweiser, Singapore has Tiger, and Thailand has Singha, and so on and so on – these are international brands of beer recognised all around the globe. Most developed countries have one such brand, or more than one. The exception, of course, has been the UK.

Representing a tied estate of one, The Jerusalem Tavern, Clerkenwell, London.

St Peter's HQ; not exactly a purpose-built brewery.

As I travelled around the world on Interbrand business, I was constantly surprised at the lack of distribution of British, and particularly English beer brands. The diet of beer drinkers everywhere seemed to be lager, lager and more lager, and every product seemed to be like all the others. In a blind tasting, I didn't think many consumers could readily distinguish Japanese Sapporo from Brazilian Brahma from Canadian Moosehead. Packaging and promoted brand image set them apart from each other but where, I wondered, was a full-tasting, English-style ale? If they were happy to drink something as wacky as Guinness, Ireland's international beer brand, why not English bitter?

We have Lobster Pots, Pint Pots, Potters' Arms, Potter's Wheels, Mustard Pots, Pepper Pots and Glue Pots. There are two Cat and Custard Pots, pinching a made-up name from a novel by Robert S Surtees called *Handley Cross*, this being the name given to the inn favoured by the fictional foxhunter Mr Jorrocks. There are three pubs in Co Durham named after that local literary and sporting figure Surtees, and two elsewhere named after Jorrocks, which makes seven for a novelist, which can't be bad.

The **Pot at Wot**, Westbury-on-Trym, Bristol, was once a post office. Post Office. At Westbury On Trym. Geddit?

Less than two per cent of Britain's beer production was exported and much of that was to Calais, to be brought straight home again by the booze cruisers. Holland exported 70 per cent of its beer. Why were British brewers seemingly ignoring the rest of the world? The answer, I thought, must lie in the historical structure of our pub and brewing trade.

Cadbury, manufacturers of sweets and chocolates, do not own sweet shops and Hovis, bakers of bread, do not own baker's shops. Yet, for generations, British brewers had produced most of the beer consumed in Britain and sold this beer to British drinkers through their own pubs. This situation was unique in the world. In no other country did the brewers control the retailing of beer. Indeed, in some countries such as the USA, it was and is illegal for brewers to own bars and sell directly to the public.

The British system, known as the tied-house system, grew up in the Nineteenth Century, a time when the brewers had massive political clout (members of the House of Lords were often called the Beerage rather than the Peerage) and it proved a very successful business formula. Prices were kept high, competition was minimised and the profits rolled in. Managing a pub on behalf of a brewer was often a relatively easy number because there was money around, the brewers wanted an easy life and they did not wish to get too involved in the day-to-day business of pub management. Everybody was happy apart from, arguably, the customers but even they tolerated the system, mainly because they did not know any better.

Until the late 1980s, a majority of Britain's pubs and bars were owned by the brewery companies and, as these tended to be the higher volume pubs, mainly in city centres, the proportion of Britain's beer production sold through the tied estate was even greater. Independently owned pubs were, in the main, lower volume country pubs and smaller 'locals'.

The promotion of a brand in the USA such as Budweiser encourages people to go into a bar and ask for a Bud. As things were in this country, there was no point in going into a Whitbread house and asking for a pint of Bass because it wouldn't be there. Going into a Bass-Charrington house and asking for a bottle of Courage Imperial Stout would have been equally fruitless. British brewers in that tied estate format had, naturally enough, directed their business efforts into controlling distribution and production rather than building brands and, naturally again, they didn't have brands with which to compete in international markets.

So, the field was open. I bought a small number of historic pubs and inns on the Norfolk/Suffolk borders and began restoring them to glory, and set up a pub in Clerkenwell, The Jerusalem Tavern, while looking for a site for my brewery. I knew the efficient ideal would be an industrial unit but that wasn't what I had in mind for brand image, and I fell for a moated manor house built largely between 1280 and 1539, including stonework from the local nunnery dissolved by Henry VIII.

It all seems a blur looking back – recruiting a head brewer and a managing director, putting in planning applications, restoring pubs and now a country house hotel had been added to the portfolio, setting up the brewery in the converted medieval thatched barn – but I wasn't forgetting the master plan: the international brand.

This was why I'd bought the pubs, even though I didn't approve of the tied system. I needed shop windows for my brand, and a guaranteed outlet for production in those early days until my brand began to make international progress.

Meanwhile, I researched the name. Our brewery was in St Peter's Hall, near Bungay, Suffolk and, much to our surprise, we found that name was available everywhere. We became St Peter's Brewery and our brand name St Peter's. We had a logo designed, based on Eighteenth Century script, and a graphic device using the key of the great gatekeeper himself and the raven of the Vikings, against whom our moat had been built.

Who would be a painter man?

The Four Bars, Cardiff, The Goat and Bicycle, Cheltenham, The Old Nags Head, Monmouth, and The Pot at Wot, Bristol (see page 124) are four of a thousand or so pub signs around the country painted by the artist Rob Rowland (www.robrowland.co.uk). In the age of Photoshop and corporate identity, it is a delight to find someone earning his crust by decorating pub signs with paint and a brush. This is what Rob has to say on the subject:

The pictorial sign is a legacy of the days when people could not read or write and trades people would hang a sign outside their premises to denote their occupations. The spread of education brought about an end to this practice with a few exceptions, the main one being the pictorial pub sign.

As a sign is hung for all to see, I feel it is important to be careful with visual information, as there will usually be someone to notice if a mistake has been made. Sometimes when I am asked to produce a sign, the customer will already have an idea or I may be asked to follow an existing theme, but usually I am given a free hand. Whatever the case, some research is generally required, either to obtain accurate information or to trigger ideas. I have a reference collection to cover most subjects including monarchs, crafts, heraldry, railways, animals, costumes, armoury and countless other subjects which the pictorial might require. However, some still need further research from outside sources including the internet. Sometimes, if the completion date is not tight (which is rarely the case), the research can be a rewarding and satisfying journey in itself, discovering all sorts of obscure and curious information along the way. This can lead on to a completely different path and spark off a more original idea than was previously thought of.

In my opinion, an inn sign artist is predominantly an illustrator as opposed to a signwriter but, because the illustration or pictorial content is painted onto a signboard rather than in a book or magazine, the difference between the two often seems unclear to people. An amateurishly painted pictorial can badly let down the rest of a well-designed signing scheme as well as lowering the reputation of good inn sign artists.

There have been many high-ranking artists in the past who have painted inn signs including Walter Crane, C R Leslie, Sir John Everett Millais RA and Hogarth of course.

It is important for a sign to be hardy enough to withstand the British climate and therefore I use only high quality materials. Most signs are painted on well-prepared aluminium or exterior grade MDF. The lifespan of a sign will vary according to where it is situated, but it can last ten to fifteen years or even more in some cases. Today, with fast moving traffic and competition from other forms of dynamic advertising, a pictorial has to be more sophisticated and appealing. One may need a strong graphic approach while another requires a more sympathetic and traditional style, depending on the type of pub and the location. The great traditional British inn sign is an art form which should continue to flourish and embellish our streets and not be allowed to dissolve into the dim and distant past as so many other skills have done. As it is an Everyman's gallery for all to see and live with, it is also important that it should be done well.

Rob Rowland, pub sign painter

Although we were selling our draught beer in our pubs, our main focus had to be on bottled beer sales. Selling draught beer through the British pub chains shows little enough profit, on top of which you have the ever-present headache of empty casks. Particularly when aluminium prices are high, stolen barrels can be crushed and shipped overseas for melting down. Smaller breweries are particularly vulnerable as they do

When Queen Elizabeth I came to the throne, a great many alehouse and inn keepers were anxious to show their loyalty. Signs depicting the Virgin Queen's head appeared all over the place. Artistic endeavours did not always match the royal opinion of herself and she actually went as far as forbidding any more, in 1563, unless they followed a design that met with certain standards. Other, non-flattering signs were removed.

The **Queen's Head** at Brandeston, Suffolk, shows a handsome lady who, at first glance, might be taken for her mother, Anne Boleyn, and some other queen's heads are those of Mistress Boleyn and her successor in decapitation, Catherine Howard. Most heads are those of the queen at the time of opening, reconstruction or rededication, making around 250 in all, and approaching 500 if you add in all the Queen Victorias and other named queens, the Queen's Arms and the simple Queens.

not have sales representatives and delivery drivers quartering the country with their eyes peeled for errant empties. Over the years, hundreds of our casks have gone missing and every time we lose one cask, we lose the profit from the sale of twenty filled casks.

Besides, a beer in a bottle can have much more brand character and impact than a draught ale and, like all the British brewers before us, we could not sell draught ale in export markets. If we couldn't get empty casks back from Norwich, how could we possibly get them back from Vancouver, St Petersburg or Mexico City? We needed therefore to invest in a distinctive bottle, a purpose built bottling hall and a bottling line and, having done so, we also wanted to sell the same product into the domestic market, which meant targeting the supermarkets.

The British glass industry offers a range of serviceable bottles in brown and clear glass that can be had for reasonable money but, of course, your beer in one of these looks the same as the others. My eye fell on an antique bottle I'd bought years before, a quart bottle with a high shoulder and an oval profile, not round. Could we base our bottle on this? If we could, we would have brand heritage built in. We would have what we call in the trade 'brand texture'.

Our new bottle proved to be extremely attractive, very well liked by our customers, and sufficiently different to allow us to register it as a trademark. Coca-Cola, eat your heart out. But it was hell on the high-speed bottling line. It took us years to get that side of things right, including specifying higher and more expensive standards to the bottle maker, and realising that we would never be able to sub-contract. No bottler wants the extra bother of filling St Peter's oval bottle, so we have to do it all.

But, you say, what about the pubs we'd bought? The tied trade system had changed in the late 1980s when the government, citing lack of competition in the retailing of beer, destroyed the tie and made it illegal for brewers to own more than 2,000 pubs each. Britain's largest brewer, Bass, owned 8,000 pubs at the time and other majors such as Whitbread and Scottish & Newcastle were not far behind. All of them were obliged to offload thousands of pubs and some, Bass and Whitbread included, decided that brewing was no longer for them and got out of the business entirely.

Not surprisingly, the government's decision to separate brewing from beer retailing was screwed up by the Law of Unintended Consequences. Once the large brewers started disposing of pubs, these were mostly purchased by newly formed pub companies and by some of the smaller brewers not worried by the 2,000 pub limit. Few pubs found their way into the hands of individuals. Thus many pub landlords simply jumped from the frying pan into a fire and most who did so preferred it in the frying pan.

The new pub owners were ambitious entrepreneurs who floated their companies on the Stock Exchange and used their newfound public status to borrow huge amounts of money. They convinced investors and lenders that their business model was a sure-fire winner, underpinned by freehold assets and a steady cash flow, guaranteed. Tenants had to pay rents and were compelled to buy beer, spirits, soft drinks and other requisites only through the company, as had been the case with the brewery and the old system, except now there was a third party. The brewery wanted paying as before, but so did the third party, the pub chain company, and so prices were higher. The pub chain was not particularly interested in running pubs – this was left to the landlords – but only in collecting rents and making a turn on beer and other supplies.

The **Quiet Woman** sign, showing a headless female dressed in servant costume of indeterminate period, can be found on the East Pacific Coast Highway, Corona del Mar, California, where 'Colorado grass fed lamb, center loin thick cut swordfish and baseball steaks from the mesquite grill, sinfully rich roasted all day short ribs and caramelized Maine diver scallops are but a few of our incredible evening treats'.

Alternatively, you may prefer a pint of Pedigree and a pork pie at the Earl Sterndale Quiet Woman, just off the Roman A515 from Buxton heading towards Ashbourne. There's another at Leek, not far away, and another a bit further at Bolsover. There are silent women too, in Coldharbour, Dorset and Slaithwaite, West Yorkshire, and a Headless Woman at Tarporley, Cheshire.

It cannot be doubted that the name sprang from one of the male human's most widespread and earnest convictions, that the female of the species can remove the hind legs of donkeys without recourse to surgery. Curiously, there seem to be no pubs featuring limbless asinine. It is also a curious fact that, despite nine out of ten men being of the firm opinion that the only quiet woman is one asleep or dead, there are but half a dozen out of 55,000 pubs noting this.

The one in Dorset is supposed to remind us of the perils of loose talk, in this case a woman's gossip endangering the local smugglers operating out of the pub. The result was a choice between voluntary silence, or silence enforced by tongue removal.

Similarly, the Quiet Woman at Earl Sterndale may commemorate a nagging wife nicknamed Chattering Charteris. Her husband, the landlord of the pub, which was then called something else, finally lost his temper and sliced off the entire nagging equipment, much to the relief of his customers.

One hates to be pedantic but one must point out to the sign painter that the correct biblical quotation, from Proverbs XV i, is 'A soft answer turneth away wrath', not soft words.

Pub landlords, running pubs on behalf of the brewers, had operated in a relatively benign environment but many of the new pub companies were distinctly red in tooth and claw. They sought the maximum return and gave very little support to their tenants. Running a pub became a much more difficult occupation than previously.

In recent years, the Government has abolished the 2,000 pub ceiling but the tied-house system is now a thing of the past, apart from the relatively small pub estates of Britain's independent breweries. Moreover, hardening attitudes to drink-driving, tougher restrictions on pubs over such things as noise and a trend towards drinking at home, have also led to pub keeping becoming a much less desirable occupation. Beer sales through pubs are well down on what they used to be. The pub owning companies are having trouble servicing their debts and are bearing down on their tenants even harder. Running a pub has never been more difficult.

What qualities do you need to run a pub? Well, first of all, you need to be incredibly hard working, have little interest in a home life and be prepared to work all hours for little reward. You will probably need to get up early in the morning for deliveries, to let the service engineer in to fix your fridge, or to give access to the cleaner. By 11am you will open up and you will need to be on your best form to welcome customers.

Your beer will need to be in tip-top condition, your brasses and woodwork polished, empty casks and bottles replaced, beer lines cleaned and last night's empties put out for collection. You will then work until 11pm or later running the bar (no point in hiring too many bar staff as this will consume all your profit). Much of the evening will be spent with people you would not necessarily have chosen as your friends.

After they've gone, you will sweep up the cigarette ends on the pavement outside, remove the chewing gum thrown into the urinals, fix any toilet seats which have been ripped off, put out the cat, lock up and finally get to bed far too late, totally shattered. And you will do this seven days a week for a return, if you're lucky, of perhaps £2 per working hour for you and your partner.

If you do decide to employ staff, it is quite likely that you will lose more than just profit. Most people are delightful but for a significant minority of those who work in pubs, the lure of alcohol and of cash is simply too great. All too often alcohol is stolen (usually consumed), white spirits such as vodka and gin are diluted and cash goes missing from tills. Even the telephone is subject to misuse. We once had a quarter's phone bill for one of our pubs for £1,000. Investigations revealed that, on the manager's

No Comment in London

'As most of us remember it, the Brockley Jack was a ramshackle old tavern of low elevation, with tall chimney stacks, chiefly conspicuous for the owning brewer's name along the roof. Traditionally said to have been the home of Jack Cade, but in all likelihood merely named after him on account of his insurgent force encamped on Blackheath, it certainly formed the lurking place of Dick Turpin and other gentlemen of the road in the days of the Georges. A novel signboard affixed to the trunk of an elm tree on the forecourt was a huge bone of a mastodon brought to light whilst deepening the Croydon Canal, behind the Brockley Jack, for the construction of the Croydon Railway in the year 1836. This prehistoric relic now adorns the facade of the handsome new tavern and hotel of which the foundation stone was laid on 19th May, 1898.'

More London Inns and Taverns, Leopold Wagner, 1925

Mr Wagner, we have to tell you it was more likely named after a highwayman called Jack Law. The sign now has your typical Hollywood/pantomime highwayman with tricorn hat, mask and red coat, riding a black horse as per gentleman of the road, although Messrs Law and Turpin were far closer to your modern-day hoodie bus-station mugger than anything gentlemanly.

The owning brewer in question was Noakes of Windsor, which became Burge & Co., which stopped brewing in 1931 and was subsumed into Meux's, which joined with Friary, Holroyd and Healy to become Friary Meux, which was bought by the Ind Coope and Allsopp arm of Allied Breweries. The pub, however, did not follow the same route and was a Courage, Barclay and Simonds house for many years before being bought by Greene King.

An old painting of the original inn does show a brown object fixed to a tree which, in shape, is very like the white object now fixed at the highest point of the facade and which resembles an extremely large shoulder blade. As for Dick Turpin, well, he was a very busy chap, we know.

The Brockley Jack rather went off in modern times, it is reported, trying too hard to attract customers with big-screen TV, but has recently refurbished in a more genteel style, perhaps more in keeping with the famous little theatre it now shelters.

The **Rockford Inn** claims to be Devon's most famous pub, which cannot be disputed without a great deal of expensive opinion-polling and the invention of a unit by which fame can be measured. In any case, it looks from the outside much the same as it did in 1901, and the river East Lyn is still a spawning ground for salmon coming in from the sea at Lynmouth.

It has changed hands several times in recent years, illustrating at once its strongest and weakest point – its spectacular but remote location on the edge of Exmoor. Parts of the building are 1700s, which you can easily see in the lower bar, but it surely could not have been an inn since then. There is no passing trade and it's not on the way to anywhere, so it must always have depended on the Exmoor holiday trade, and the fishing.

day off, the stand-in barman had spent the entire evening on a sex line to Vanuatu. Such things can be pretty dispiriting.

Of course, there can be compensations. For a start you are your own boss so, in theory, you can do whatever you want, though there is not much to do when you are, metaphorically, chained to the bar. And there are some people who find the pub life terrifically good fun. They love the social contact, the variety, the sense of being at the centre of a community, the challenge of trying to grow the business, the feeling that every day

The **Rose and Crown**, Ashbury, now designated 'Hotel, bar and restaurant', is still there but without the thatch, which went sometime between 1930 and 1940 – our photograph is 1919 – and the archway for coaches is filled in too, but more recently. Like so many, it has managed to keep ahead of the game by developing what it offers way beyond any 1919 ideas of a rustic oasis. While many pub purists will sneer at the rocket-and-balsamic-vinegar set with their red onion tarts and pan-fried whatnots (what else, pray, would you fry them in?), the fact remains that without such business progress there would be far fewer village pubs for us all to go in.

There are at least 200 Rose and Crowns, the name and the sign being a simple expression of loyalty to monarch and country.

is different from the last even when common-sense tells you this is not really the case.

Once we had St Peter's sufficiently on track not to need so many shop windows, we sold all our pubs except one. In short, running pubs was too distracting in such a small operation. The little local difficulties climbed too far up the chain of command – to me. I didn't want to know about the chef who was off sick when fourteen were booked in for dinner, nor about the dignitary complaining about the singing on a Saturday night. I had a meeting once with a formidable lady chair of the parish council when I was thinking seriously about closing a small village pub, for the simple reason that it was losing a massive amount of money. This lady berated me as if I were the devil incarnate. The village had to have a pub, she said. That much must have been obvious, even to a ruthless, grasping baby-roaster and highway robber such as myself. I asked her what she thought about the pub – had we restored it well? Had we got the menu right for the locale? Oh, she didn't know. Good heavens, she never went into pubs.

I made a decision: from then on, I was going to enjoy going exclusively into other people's pubs.

A bit more about St Peter's. Our UK sales are almost all bottled beer sales to supermarkets and restaurants but, from year one, exports have formed about 40 per cent of turnover. Our major markets are the USA, Canada, Scandinavia and Russia, while other relatively important markets include Holland, France, Mexico and Japan. We are on our way to becoming something the English brewing industry has never had before: a major international brand.

John Murphy, St Peter's Brewery.

It is futile but interesting to your correspondent to speculate on what might have happened to British pubs had we not had the tied system. Might we, like the USA, have become dominated by a few, very similar brands? It couldn't have happened in the UK until recently, because draught beer wouldn't travel and we had no motorways, but you could argue that it's happening now. You could say that lager is not so much a type of beer with many varieties, but a brand in itself. As John Murphy says, consumers in blind tastings would be hard put to tell one ordinary-strength lager from another. Similarly, the pasteurised, filtered, bright, bland, thoroughly undistinguished beers going under the generic name of smooth, are so clearly distinguished from real beer that they could also be grouped together and called a brand.

Perhaps the very regime that prevented us having an international brand, the tied-house system that made brewers concentrate on brewing local beer for local people, has given us that vital element of the pub, the interesting product at the bar. We may complain frequently and bitterly about things not being what they were, and we may sometimes complain about the beer, but surely we are better off for not having Hobson's choice between bottles of Bud or Michelob or, for that matter, Miller's 'Real draft' in bottles. Perhaps, in an age when a car-boot lid can be advertised as intelligent and capable of delivering flexible loading solutions, we should not be too surprised at real draught beer, pasteurised, filtered four times, in a bottle.

You can buy bottled beer from the Earl Soham Brewery too, but that's not what motivates founder John Bjornson. He shares a love of good British bitter beer with John Murphy, but has come at the business from a completely different direction. A chemist by education and wanting to get into brewing in the late 1970s, the only job Bjornson could get was in a maltings. The firm sent him to brewing school, he made a lot of friends in the trade, he studied the workings and results of the laboratory pilot plants that all the big brewers had and, in 1984, he bought a pub, with an ancient annexe that looked like it might have been a brewhouse once, from the now defunct company Tolly Cobbold.

'My ambition then was very simple. I wanted to brew the kind of beer I liked, and I wanted to sell it in the pub, with any surplus, if I had any, going to beer festivals and maybe the odd free house. Of course,

Cider inside her inside

There used to be two types of cider widely available. You could get bottled cider, sweet or dryish, in screw-top quart flagons, made by Bulmer's, Gaymer's and so on, and you could get draught and bottled scrumpy, the rough farmhouse cider not generally available outside the West Country and some southern counties such as Kent.

Sweet bottled cider has become a popular drink in pints with much ice, largely through the advertising of the Irish firm Magner's. Sweet cider has long been a popular drink in Ireland. Not every Irish person likes the bitterness of Guinness.

Draught ciders with character, made from apples, such as James White or Aspall in Suffolk and Thatcher's in Devon and Somerset, compete with nationally advertised brands made from imported apple-juice concentrate. Connoisseurs will say the only true cider is the scrumpy, farmhouse cider, flat, cloudy, and so dry it will take the enamel off your teeth, but be warned.

There is an excellent pub just outside Branscombe, east Devon, called The Fountain Inn. Here, the lady wife complained that her half of farmhouse cider tasted awful, and it did. It had gone off. You could have pickled onions in it. A taking back thereof resulted only in comments implying that the ignorant and effete tourist shouldn't try to drink proper farmhouse cider, and an offer of a half of Strongbow instead. This experience was repeated almost exactly in the Hare and Hounds, Putts Corner on the Honiton-Sidmouth road, with added backchat from customers at the bar and no offer of replacement.

everybody I knew in the pub world said I was crackers. I could sell my beer in my own pub but I'd never sell it anywhere else, against the local gods of real ale, Adnams.'

The pub was The Victoria in Earl Soham, a Suffolk village not far from Framlingham. It was a small two-roomer, which looked like it had never been touched by the dreaded moderniser's hand (and it still does – wonderful). The annexe had had chickens in it but, with second-hand brewing vessels from the recently deceased Brightlingsea Brewery and some inspirational plumbing design from John, it did the job.

More than 550 Royal Oaks makes this the second most used name. In Fishguard stands the one in which the treaty of surrender was signed by the foolish French who had tried to invade, landing nearby at Llanwnda in 1797. Numbers of Welsh women in traditional costume of red cloak and tall black hat had, at a distance, looked like a regiment of redcoats and the ragtag French mixture of reprobates surrendered without firing a shot. One

woman in particular, Jemima Nicholas, rounded up a dozen of them and she was armed only with a pitchfork.

Mostly the sign depicts the tree with the young Prince Charles, later Charles II, and his companion Colonel Carless, hiding in it from the Parliament army after the Royalist defeat at the Battle of Worcester, 1651. After the restoration of the monarchy, Charles's birthday, May 29, was declared Royal Oak Day and a great many alehouses, taverns and inns renamed themselves, partly through patriotic enthusiasm and partly because it's a jolly good story.

The **Royal Oak**, Winsford, in the Exmoor National Park, pictured here in 1950, still has its thatch as befits a Twelfth Century farmhouse and offers rooms with four-poster beds. The ford is over the juvenile, dashing River Exe, which has a long way to go to Exeter, where there are three more Royal Oaks.

'I had a rough idea of what I was looking for in a beer. I don't like strong beers and I don't like dark beers. I wanted it light, bitter, a certain kind of floral note but not too much, and I hit it first time. Victoria Bitter was the result and I've stuck with it.'

That was in 1985 and there were a lot more free houses in those days. John's beer gradually built a reputation. He bought another pub too, the derelict Station Hotel in Framlingham, and the chicken shed was outgrown.

'I was thinking about moving the brewery elsewhere but the bank manager said that the Earl Soham Brewery, now a well-known name, should be in Earl Soham, and he offered to lend me enough money to buy the old village garage. So, we fitted it out with more second-hand kit and we're still there. The difference now is that we use barley from Brandeston, down the road, and hops from Sibton, only a few miles further, so we're entirely local.'

The pub chains were buying up the free houses and imposing tight contracts on their tenants, who had to buy from the preferred lists. Any back-dooring and they were in breach. Even so, John Bjornson found more and more markets.

'We swapped guest beers with other small brewers, and we trialled an unknown cyder with a y, Aspall, in The Victoria and The Station, which

> ### *Pub Rubbish Korner*
>
> 'What's not to like about this historically rich pub that was once the local of our most famous admiral? It oozes traditional charm with stone-flagged floors and friendly locals. If the smell of the barbecue doesn't hook your nostrils, then you've got appetite issues.'
>
> This adolescent drivel is courtesy of *The Guardian*, concerning The Lord Nelson, Burnham Thorpe, which is indeed an excellent pub deserving of serious and proper description. If anyone knows what appetite issues are, please explain while oozing traditionally all over the stone-flagged locals and friendly floors.

The Ship Inn, Porlock, claims to have been established in the Thirteenth Century and that may be so. We can say that the exterior is the same as it was in 1901, when our photograph was taken, and that it remains a popular and stately pleasure dome to this day. S T Coleridge, an expert on pleasure domes, albatrosses and other matters, lived in nearby Nether Stowey and, according to some authorities, was writing *Kubla Khan* in The Ship when he was famously interrupted by 'a person on business from Porlock'.

While the saying, 'a man from Porlock' or just 'a Porlock', has come to mean any literary interruption, it must throw doubt on The Ship as the venue. It would have been unnecessary so to designate the person's home town if Coleridge was in The Ship. More likely, if he was in a pub, it might have been The George or The Rose and Crown in Nether Stowey, or The Ancient Mariner, which Coleridge would have known as The First and Last.

Not counting those pubs named after particular ships, or those called the something ship or the ship and something, there are about 250 plain ships and old ships, some by the sea and some a long way from it. It is tempting to speculate that a portion of these landlubbery ships were originally shippons (or shippens), the old word for cowsheds. There are plenty of ploughs, wheatsheaves, barley mows, dun cows and jolly farmers (the latter mainly on pub signs rather than in real life) so, in more agricultural days, we might have popped down to the cowshed for a pint.

As trade moved upmarket, maybe the cowshed wasn't the most inviting place and so it became a ship but nowadays, when hardly anybody knows anything at all about cows and their sheds, the byre has returned. If you're in The Wirral, you can go to a fairly recently converted barn which has been reborn as The Shippons Inn, Irby.

we now had open. Aspall was an old family firm that had fallen into disrepair, to be reinvigorated by the latest and eighth generation of the family, the Chevalliers. Beer and cider together in our van made a more attractive offer to the free trade and we both benefited, and Aspall has gone on to great success.

'We always seemed to be able to sell as much beer as we could produce. I've never been in this to make a fortune. I've just had this naive belief that there will always be enough people who want proper beer. Mind you, if I could get my casks back I'd be a lot better off. I don't know how many I've bought over the years but I'm sure I've lost more than I have now.'

When Young's closed the Wandsworth brewery, John couldn't believe it. How could a firm like that sell their birthright for a mess of new office blocks, or whatever? Somehow this gave him the impetus to strike a kind of reverse blow and, after two years' negotiating, he was able to lease part of the old and vacant Tolly Cobbold brewery in Ipswich, along with the pub, The Brewery Tap.

'Here we installed yet another second-hand plant but this time one designed and built by engineers and steam driven, not bodged together by me and driven by Bunsen burners. We're brewing six different beers. The tied system of the pub chains is relaxing a little so we can get in there more easily, and I've watched young people get fed up with lager and switch to proper beer. It's cheaper as well. I think it's the only growth market.'

We, the public, can only watch and admire. Bjornson hasn't gone the microbrewery, niche market, specialist beer route. He's taken on the established brewers at their own game, making old-fashioned draught beer that people drink as a regular thing, down the pub, but he won't be taking them on in the matter of tied estate. That's another view he shares with John Murphy. He's been lucky to find good people to run the three pubs he has but he's stopping there.

Murphy's comments about what it takes to run a pub do not mention paperwork, which is a great bane of publicans' lives, especially under the new licensing system with all its form-filling but, as he says, it used to be a relatively benign environment. To prove this, let us hear the true story of a certain publican in kinder times.

This chap had inherited the tenancy from his father in 1943, father having had it since 1882. After twenty-odd years running the pub, our man received a letter, out of the blue, from Her Majesty's Inland Revenue. This letter invited him to file a tax return.

His reaction was a simple one. He had never done such a thing, nor had his father before him, and so he didn't see why he should start now. In any case, as he explained to a friend and customer who was an accountant, he had never made a profit so he didn't need to pay any tax.

His habit, as was the case with many publicans, was to pay all his outgoings from the till. This was everything, from brewery to bread man to cigarette rep to cleaning lady. He did have a bank account because some people paid him with cheques and a few wanted paying by cheque, but the balance in it hardly varied from one year-end to the next, which was incontrovertible evidence for the lack of profitability.

The landlord was at length persuaded by his friend, the accountant, that it would be wise to comply with Her Majesty's wishes-by-proxy, and so a set of accounts was drawn up, based on information supplied. The polite accounting term for this information would have been 'incomplete records'. Eventually realising that no more facts or figures would be forthcoming for a year in which the bank balance had gone down from £800 to £700, thus proving that a loss had been made, never mind a profit, the accountant prepared the accounts for signing off and arranged a ceremony in the bar.

As he and the landlord sat with pen, papers and pints, a workman drew up outside in a badly bruised old lorry, and came into the pub asking for cash 'for the bricks'.

'Bricks?' said the accountant to the landlord. 'Cash for the bricks? From the till, I assume?'

'That's all right,' said the landlord. 'This is not to do with the pub. I'm building a bungalow for my retirement.'

Who Goes In?

In the face of a century of competition from the cinema, then the wireless, then the television, plus the working men's clubs and the cheap booze from the supermarkets and the smoking ban – well, it must say something about the attractions of the pub that anyone goes in at all.

Leslie Forse, once editor of *The Morning Advertiser*, the publican's trade paper, defined the pub as 'The haunt of the common man … the citizen who, whatever his rank or position, meets other citizens as equals at the bar.' This was certainly the case when 'meet', 'citizens' and 'bar' were the key words. In Mr Forse's time, pubs were mostly places to which people went in expectation of taking part in a social act.

Perhaps now there is more of an expectation of being entertained, of the pub providing something easily digestible, such as TV sport or live music,

The New **Soldier Dick** in Furness Vale, Derbyshire, is one of those built on the site of a much older inn, has a new sign and has reverted to plain Dick. The soldier was wounded and given shelter by the innkeeper, whose wife nursed him back to full strength. It seems that he was such a good story-teller that he was given permanent quarters at the inn in return for attracting and entertaining customers. A very similar story is said to explain the name of The 

Scotch Piper, at Lydiate between Liverpool and Southport, previously a Royal Oak and allegedly the oldest pub in Lancashire. If it is the oldest, it will surely predate Charles II and so must have had another name before that.

The **Speculation Inn** at Hundleton, on the B4320 a couple of miles west of Pembroke, was a cottage until 1840 or thereabouts when entrepreneurs speculated that an alehouse would do well in an area not over endowed with same. The rabbit catchers of south Pembs were grateful too when it soon became the rabbit hub. They dropped off their hauls and had a pint or two, knowing that the Pembroke tannery

cart would be along to pick up all their bunny skins. The new sign shows local farmer and famous rider John James on Cromwell, prize horse and film star.

There is one other pub in the UK called The Speculation, in Speculation Place, Washington, Tyne and Wear. The name may have come from the coal-mining industry, possibly connected with the hopeful sinking of exploratory shafts, looking for coal seams.

No Comment in London

'Concerning the Cock at Highbury, there is nothing to say save that the ancient inn was demolished to make way for the North London Railway Station, and its successor merely flanks the wide courtyard which accommodated the coaches and carriers' waggons that drew up at its portals.'

More London Inns and Taverns, Leopold Wagner, 1925

The station, commissioned in 1872, was a magnificent building in a kind of Victorian Norman style with a touch of mad Italian Gothic. The south wing of it was the new pub, which took a hit from a flying bomb in 1944. The whole lot was demolished in the 1960s and rebuilt in the insane Visigoth-brutalist style of that period. The 'famous' pub now has one giant screen and four TVs showing non-stop Sky sports, also four fruit machines and has, according to one report, an amazing atmosphere when Arsenal are involved. It would seem that Mr Wagner could not see into the future or he might have realised how well off he was with the railway station.

rather than something you have to contribute towards. At a pub in Leeds called The Newlands, now gone, some Saturday nights of 40 years ago would erupt into singing from the customers, not from a band. One quite elderly lady used to get up on a table to sing, almost intelligibly, about her brother, Sylvest, and her sister, Mae West, who wore a pair of saucepan lids on her chest (BIG CHEST). Someone else would roll a silver dollar, down upon the ground and it would ro-ho-hole because it's row-how-hound. A man, without a woman, is like a ship, without a sail, a boat, without a rudder, or a fish without a tail. A man, without a woman, is like a ship, upon the sand. But if there's one thing worse in this universe then it's a woman, it's a woman, it's a woman without a man.

The extent to which those nights were enjoyed can be judged by the fact that your correspondent has never heard those songs sung since and yet, 40 years on, the words can be recalled without a moment's hesitation. They were good times, hugely enjoyed by everyone there, and you never quite knew when they would happen or why. Maybe it was just because somebody turned up who could play the piano.

'The clever men at Oxford,
Know all there is to be knowed.
But they none of them know one half as much
As intelligent Mr Toad.'

The Wind in the Willows, Kenneth Graham.

And he looks it, doesn't he? Sitting there as he has for eons on top of his outcrop, turned into sandstone by a wicked witch, or possibly just eroded by the weather, Toad of Rust Hall, rather than Toad Hall, attracts gawkers in their thousands, many of whom feel obliged, naturally, to drop into The Toad Rock Retreat, Rusthall, Tunbridge Wells.

Other Toads in the UK are few, apart from the Slurping Toad chain which are, perhaps, pubs in a slightly different sense from the old definition. Two Toad Halls, in Saltburn and Rhos, a

Lazy Toad in Shoreham, a Tipsy Toad in Bulkington, and that's about it unless you want to pull on your daisies, run down the apples, cross the frog and dive into the old rubba for a larf, or patronise the Frog and Toads of Gillingham and Bristol.

The Vintners' Company and the Dyers' Company, two powerful London trade guilds originating in Medieval times, share rights in swan-upping with the monarch. This ancient privilege, all to do with who was allowed to eat swan and who wasn't, is carried on ceremonially today, mainly as a very

good way to keep tabs on the swan population while taking a few glasses of wine. Those un-ringed swans upped by the monarch's uppers are returned un-ringed, thus remaining in the monarch's gift. Other un-ringed swans are given one leg ring by the Dyers' men or two by the Vintners.

In the old days, they didn't use rings. They cut marks, five for the monarch, one for the Dyers, two for the Vintners, on the swans' beaks and, as the Vintners were permitted to sell wine in taverns without a licence until Edward VI revoked that right and, as the Vintners' coat of arms featured two swans, some of those taverns, and some inns dealing with the Company, would have been certain to take a swan into their name.

The **Swan with Two Necks** was a sign first seen in London, in the 1500s. The Canterbury post was calling twice a week at The Two Necked Swan near Billingsgate in 1637. The name is said to be a corruption by ignorant sign painters of the Vintners' upped swans, those with two nicks. The learned gentleman who first put forth this theory, in 1810, was Sir Joseph Banks, the botanist who accompanied Captain Cook, and who are we to argue with him?

If it was a sign painter's mistake, it would have to have been the first one, the first time anyone suggested calling a tavern The Swan With Two Nicks. All sign painters thereafter would have had to follow because nobody has ever seen a sign for a pub called The Swan with Two Nicks or, for that matter, The Two Nicked Swan.

Such painting errors do not seem likely. Some artists go to school and learn to spell. Some, commissioned to paint Two Nicks, would have done so. Some, likewise commissioned but painting Necks, would have been made to correct their mistake by their irate commissioners.

Also, the problem remains of what else a painter might put on his sign apart from the name. A close-up of a beak with two scratches would hardly inspire so, given the feelings of liberty and adventure that may grip a painter when confronted by a difficult problem, would not a swan with two glorious curved necks be more fun?

Possibly, but we still have that annoying little fact that there has never been a pub with Nicks, as far as we know. Travellers returning from South America in those earliest days would tell of a swan with a white body and a black neck (*Cygnus melanchoryphus*, if you want to know). How easily that could be translated into a swan with two necks. Or, travellers returning from the east might tell of a two-headed phoenix that ate only dewdrops. Well, that's no dafter than the two nicks story.

The double neck pictured is in Langdon, north of Birmingham; there are about ten more. The Billingsgate Two Necked Swan, by Sommers Quay, not far from Pudding Lane, disappeared in the Great Fire of London. The Two Necked Swan in Great Yarmouth closed in 2007 but there's a Swan with Two Knecks in Chorley, for which spelling there is no etymology and so we might suggest an errant sign painter.

At The Dennison Arms, Ayton, near Scarborough, in the same era, things were more organised. Little Eric, and later Irish George, were paid to play the piano, and people came from miles around. A few of the customers helped out with organisation, so everyone could be found a seat somehow, and the songs ranged from choral hymns like *Steal away* and *How great thou art* to music hall numbers and some faintly vulgar ones such as *The German Clockwinder*. Every Saturday and Sunday, certain elements of the procedure would be repeated. The landlord's father always sang about somebody throwing tomatoes. 'Tomatoes don't hurt, he replied with a grin. Well, these buggers did cos they were in the tin, singing tooralaiy-ay, tooralaiy-ay, tooralaiy-tooralaiy-tooralaiy-ay.' A tall fellow known only as Hands would do an Al Jolson impression. Those who were not Leeds United supporters would happily join in with 'What do you get when you follow Leeds? You only get lies, and pain, and sorrow. So for at least, until tomorrow I-I-I-I-I'll never follow Leeds again.'

Nights like these were not general practice, even that long ago. If there ever was a time when everyone gathered around the piano at the drop of a hat, in every village and town, every night, making their own entertainment in those days by singing 'Knees up on Ilkley Moor, down at the Old Lambeth Walk', well, your ancient correspondent never knew it.

But, nights like that filled pubs and sold beer in great quantities. Knowing this full well, a young but sensible landlord in a seaside town in Devon recently installed a piano in his pub. He would normally have no music at all, no

The **Triple Plea**, slightly stranded on the old road out of Halesworth in the Beccles/Bungay direction, is the only one of its kind and its sign tells an entire story on its own – but one which is open to interpretation.

There's the old boy, lying pale and wan in his death bed, while the priest pleads for his soul. That much looks fairly sure, and the godly pleas would appear as if they might be in vain, given the proximity of the great ungodly, Beelzebub himself, waiting to claim his own. No wonder the old chap looks pale as he recounts his sins.

Meanwhile, our learned friend is also making a plea – for what? Is he representing someone who wants the will changed before it's too late? Is he – somewhat unsympathetically – pointing out a legal tangle with the will, an earthly matter that needs rectifying but which can hardly concern a man who, by the look of him, has only a few minutes to live. Or is the lawyer, in full wig and gown, pleading for a signature to give himself power over the estate?

The doctor's bill is on the table, with a pen. Or is it a bill? Some authorities say it is a document of permission to be granted by the old man for his body to be used for the benefit of medical science. Has the old boy already signed it? Is the doctor checking the pulse to see if it's time to call the blood waggon?

piped music anyway, and certainly no television unless it was the Six Nations or England football, but his idea failed because a piano player could not be found in the town, or at least one who could play songs for singing drinkers, or wanted to.

Still, there was always the conversation, which is really the crux of the matter. At a pub in Cumbria, high in the hills where the wild things are, a court report in the local paper was being discussed. A farmer, well known to most of the people in the pub, had been up before the beak, accused of sheep rustling.

It should be explained to town-dwellers that there could hardly be a more heinous crime in those districts, where fences are few. Being caught in bed with a neighbour's wife would be as nought compared to stealing his sheep.

May 1790

I breakfasted, dined, supped and slept again at the Angel Inn at Yarmouth, as did likewise my Brother and Wife, Mrs R Clarke and Nancy. As soon as we had breakfasted we got into the Yarmouth Coaches again and took a ride on the Beach, called at a public House on the Coast and had some refreshment, and returned home to our Inn to dinner. Paid and gave the public House on the Beach 0.2.0. At a Pot-House on the Quay with my brother amongst some jolly Tars, for Porter 0.0.4.

(next day) We then returned to our Inn and dined on some cold Meat and Sallad and some Tarts. My Brother did not go with us, but went out by himself and did not return till we had almost dined; he had been out with some Tars and had been drinking with them and was a little merry.

The Diary of a Country Parson, James Woodforde

The Angel Inn dated from the mid 1600s and was on the Market Place, by Howard Street. Its licence was removed next door to The Prince Regent in 1939, and during the war it served as a British Restaurant. It was demolished in 1957. The Prince Regent became a Henekey Inn before closing in 1981.

In other sheepish areas the same attitude occurs, to the extent that some pubs, for instance The Skirrid, near Abergavenny, claim to have had a sheep-stealer hanged in the bar. That particular hanging is said to have been in 1110, whereas The Skirrid's earliest bits were built in the mid-1600s, so it is very probable that the only items of flesh and bone suspended from those Welsh beams were hams.

Anyway, the Cumbrian man had pleaded guilty and asked for a number of other offences over the years to be taken into consideration. Reading from the newspaper, one customer quoted, 'and his lawyer, in his defence, said that his behaviour was inexplicable.'

'What does inexplicable mean?' said Ralph the mole-catcher. Joe the gypsy replied, 'It's same as when you shit yourself.'

Joe was a member of a small class of pub goers that observant landlords and landladies identify and cultivate. Good pubs have several Joes who come in at different times, but their function is the same. They are the pub's wits, the central characters, the ones whom strangers love to meet and listen to, the ones whom regulars hope will be there when they go in.

The fortunate pub has a number of secondary ones too, that is, people who can hold their own, give it and take it, and who are personalities in their own right if not quite so dominant as The One. Some unfortunate pubs have a

There are about 50 Welcomes and Welcome Inns and, among the Welcome variations, one Sailor, one To Town, one To Gower, one Hand, one Home, and five Strangers, three of them in Sussex, which is where this one is, at Crowborough.

There are about 60 Griffins, including a couple of Griffin's Heads, and around 350 White Horses (see page 104), both being much used in heraldry, but there's only one **White Horse and Griffin**. It's in Whitby old town, is 200 years old, and much admired these days as a restaurant.

subsidiary variety of central character who actually believes himself to be The One and who relishes the role to such an extent that everybody else wishes he would shut up. He makes the assumption that all are fascinated by every word he says, and that all agree with his political views which are, substantially, those that might have been expressed by *The Daily Mail* in 1485.

Also boring, but without the extraversion, is the one with no conversation except a detailed description of something that happened at work or on the golf course. Sometimes the two are combined, so you are obliged to listen to the many detailed problems associated with stripping down a 1956 Briggs and Stratton that had never been serviced, followed by the wind-affected dog-leg on the eleventh which would have won the game had it not been for picking a seven iron instead of a six for the second shot and so falling ten yards short of that small area of the fairway where the ball tends to roll on with the slope and give you a perfect angle for the green. As it was, there was no option but to … oh, yes, thanks, just a half.

A fine example of this occurred when a reasonably famous actress came into the pub, a very good-looking reasonably famous actress, wearing a very low cut dress. All the men gathered round her as she began describing her role in the latest West End production, in minute detail, step by step and word by word, with accompanying explanations and frequent use of the first person singular pronoun. She had to stop to go to the loo. When she came back, her crowd of admirers had dispersed and were all earnestly engaged in new conversations. The poor girl burst into tears.

There are some who like telling jokes but can never keep one going in a straight line. There are some who are masters or mistresses of the verbal feint, parry and thrust, so sharp that sometimes the victim doesn't realise he's been cut. There are the interrupters, who cannot help referring every turn and angle of conversation back on themselves, so if you are relating your adventures when you went white-water rafting in New Zealand, the interrupter will mention the rowing boat episode involving mother-in-law on the lake in Peasholm Park. If you are describing the time you accidentally bumped into Prince Phillip in the beer tent and knocked him over, the interrupter will cut in at a crucial point with personal views on the monarchy as a sustainable means of governance.

However, this is a pub, not a private dinner party in your house, so the rotten joke teller will be told to get to the point. Interrupters will be offered more and more difficult subjects to try to relate to self, until they give up when you tell the story of your brother, the call girl and the penguin.

Stereotypes such as The Major do exist, cuddling their halves of bitter in behandled glasses to their doubtless bemedalled chests, and the rugger bugger, and the old soak, and the nothing's as good as it was grump, but these can also be the bore or the rapier wit or, for that matter, the fantasist. One example of this latter type that springs to mind was the pork butcher, famous for his pies, who claimed to have been on the submarine that sank the *Belgrano*. Even if he had been seconded to the Royal Navy from MI5 at the age of eleven, this man was so fat that he would never have got down the hatch. His story set off a series of James Bond jokes, featuring The Pie Who Loved Me, Live and Let Pie, The Man with the Golden Pie and so forth (well, yes, you did have to be there really). Another fantasist in a different pub claimed to have missed out on actually being James Bond because he was late for the screen test, and by the time he got to it they had already given the job to George Lazenby.

All human life is there, except the extremes and, generally, except for anything bad. Pub goers are a convivial, pleasant lot, as a rule, and the electrician mixes

Although this sign in Disley interprets the lion literally, and in a rather spooky way, the widespread use of it is, like so many pub names, connected with heraldry and therefore with kings or local nobility. Edward IV and the Dukes of Norfolk are just two of the high born who emblazon this beast, a symbol of power and virtue, and something like 160 pubs are named for it.

The Disley Lion is recently refurbished and offers eight real ales, including a strong mild. Such choice is not unique but very much more rare than it should be. One novel good idea at the Lion is the dog room, with water, food and hitching.

with the farmer who mixes with the retired solicitor who mixes with the lady novelist. In this writer's pub we probably have an above-average number of artistic types, university professors, gold shippers and devout lesbians, but you get that sort of thing in country districts not too far from London. We also have an antique dealer known as Lovejoy, a delightful lady cafe owner, builders, plumbers, tree surgeons, horse dealers, the vicar comes in on a Tuesday, a school dinner lady keeps hens and supplies us with eggs, there's a chap who runs a mail-order clothing firm, another who sells things to Russians, several old boys who've been there since the grass grew, and so on and so on.

If you want anything, there'll be someone who can get it or do it, or who knows someone who can. Venison? Hay? New barge boards on your house? Logs? Rotavator? Website design?

And finally, let us consider those who, for a good reason or another, find themselves to be elephant's, Brahms, or bitten by a barn weasel and refusing to fight. If one should find oneself in that state of being as inebriated as any of certain aquatic salamanders, one should remember to tell the constable that, actually, the correct expression is 'as an ewt'. The proper word is ewt, not newt, and it's only slurring the words together that has got us to 'a newt' from, constable, as I said, 'an ewt'.

Not a lot of police officers know that.

> ### *Pub Rubbish Korner*
>
> The Duke of York in Whitby, claimed *The Daily Telegraph*, was 'often patronised by Bram Stoker'. This is not a claim The Duke's management would seriously make themselves, except to have a bit of fun at innocent journalists' expense.
>
> As one who went to school in Whitby in the 1950s, where local history – Captain Cook, St Hilda, Caedmon, the Penny Hedge, the jet industry, the Viking heritage – was heavily emphasised, this writer can tell you that Bram Stoker and Dracula were never mentioned. Never.
>
> Stoker was an Irish writer who lived most of his working life in London. If he came to Whitby at all, it was on holiday, once, possibly in 1890. He may have gone to the Duke of York, of course, although he never found it necessary to go to a pub or any other place in Transylvania. This whole Dracula thing is an exaggerated Whitby tourist trick recently cooked up and swallowed whole by the likes of *The Daily Telegraph*.

The pub quiz

In the right spirit, a pub quiz is a wonderful thing, a sporting competition with no sweat or injury, with a prize largely consisting of honour alone and the opportunity of taking the waters while you're doing it. In the wrong spirit, it can cause a riot.

Cheating in pub games is a fact of life. We've all seen the killer grannies of the British Legion club dominating the dominoes by means of scratched noses, lifted eyebrows, one, two or three fingers extended and heavy clearing of throats. The same sort of thing happens in quizzes, generally to do with illicit foreknowledge of the questions or an especially one-eyed quizmaster.

An instance of the former occurred when the landlady of a certain pub, let's call it the Bungay Fleece, rang up our landlord to say that the questions for next Sunday's quiz league match had been opened by mistake and accidentally perused. The offer was to send the questions over so that we could have a look at them, and that would make us even, wouldn't it? Our landlord tried to make sense of this but failed. Instead he suggested that, as there was no time to order new questions, The Fleece would have to field a second team of people who were not privy to the answers. This was agreed.

First question, to The Fleece. Who said 'I think, therefore I am'? The Fleece answer was Pierre-Joseph Proudon. Wrong. Over to us. We knew it was Descartes. Correct. Our question. Who said 'Property is theft'? We didn't

Traditional Cornish mussels become moules, 'marinière-d' in an entirely new way, with two quid added on for traditional chips for the coach trippers.

However, the more we do away with things traditional, the more we use the word. On signs we can see that we have traditional markets, traditional Sunday lunches, traditional fish and chips and, here in Pembrokeshire and many other places, we have a traditional country pub. **The Wolfe**, of course, is named for the general of that name who was killed while winning Canada for the Empire.

Outside a pub in Derbyshire your correspondent saw an A-board with the words 'Traditional Fayre Food'; answers on a postcard, please, to The Eagle, Market Square, Buxton. The word traditional is from Latin roots meaning to hand over or give across, and has come to signify that which is handed down, such as a long established custom, belief or practice, especially by word of mouth. Sunday lunch, fish and chips, the market and the pub, and all the other aspects of our lives to which bright sparks have added the word traditional, by their very nature have no need of the word, especially in writing, and must arouse suspicion where used.

know but we could have a jolly good guess. Er, how about Pierre-Joseph Proudon. Correct. And so on. If only The Fleece team had read the questions and answers a little earlier on that mistaken night, their memories would have been better and they would have matched question with answer more often. As it was, we won.

The town of Stalybridge, Cheshire, is quite unlike any other in its pubs. For a start, it has a station buffet, built in 1885, that functions as a pub and has all the Victorian atmospheric qualities plus a goodly spreading of the Manchester, Sheffield and Lincolnshire Railway. Food available there includes Lancashire black peas, called carlins in Cumbria and the north-east, where they are eaten once a year on the Sunday before Palm Sunday, and in Yorkshire where they are fed to pigeons.

Stalybridge also has the pub with the longest name, and the pub with the shortest. There can be no argument with a one-letter name for The Q, which is almost next door to the railway station. There used to be a pub called The X, not far from Cullompton in Devon, but it changed its name to The Merry Harriers and so Q rules. Meanwhile, the longest name does cause a bit of discussion.

At the time of writing, one of the erstwhile contenders, The Shoulder of Mutton and Cucumbers (31 letters) at Yapton, Sussex, is the subject of a planning request with listed building consent, to turn it into two private houses. Another, The White Heifer That Travelled, 27 letters, is in Darlington and, being new, has clearly missed an opportunity, when The Old White Heifer That Travelled A Considerable Distance In Days Of Yore might have pushed it to the front. The Henry J Bean's

THE LONGEST NAMED PUB IN GREAT BRITAIN
THE OLD THIRTEENTH CHESHIRE ASTLEY VOLUNTEER RIFLEMAN CORPS INN

But His Friends All Call Him Hank Bar And Grill, 52 letters, of Chelsea and Wimbledon, equally clearly had no intention of missing any opportunity at all but has missed it. Henry Jehosophat Bean would have been enough, or Bar And Brasserie but, in any case, being part of an international American ribs and burger franchise, or possibly a burgerz 'n' ribz dinerama, it cannot qualify within the meaning of the pub as defined in the constitution of Great Britain and Ireland.

The winner, therefore, has to be Stalybridge's own The Old Thirteenth Cheshire Astley Volunteer Rifleman Corps Inn, 55 letters, known locally as The Rifleman. The Astley part of the name refers to John Astley, 1724-1787, a portrait painter with a reputation for seducing his wealthy female sitters. One such was the widowed Lady Dukinfield-Daniel, of Gorse Hall on the hill above Stalybridge, who is supposed to have told Astley that if she liked the portrait he could have the original. They married, he spent a large part of her fortune on excessive living, but did a few good works including helping to form the Thirteenth Cheshire Volunteers. She died, he inherited and moved to London, where he went mad. A few of the portraits he made are still around but his only really worthwhile and substantial memorial is a solid-looking pub in Stalybridge.

Everybody hates the professionals, the team that comes together just to win and tours all the town's pubs' quiz nights, and the charity quizzes too. One such, in Buxton, Derbyshire, went every Sunday to The Sun Inn to win the four pints of beer and dinner for two, and the name under which they entered was 'Eat and Drink Free at The Sun'.

Quiz leagues also can be serious business, as when The New Inn, Hoff, near Appleby-in-Westmorland, played host in a league match to the much-respected Golden Ball, of Appleby. The Golden Ball always won the league, except when the schoolteachers of the Kirkby Stephen White Lion won it. The New Inn team liked to think we were a natural third.

Our home quiz inquisitor was a retired gentleman of dapper and immaculate appearance, with a voice that combined the mellifluence, accents and carrying powers of the two great theatrical Donalds; Wolfit and Sinden. He relished his role as master of ceremonies and, usually, was very good at it, but on this occasion he'd had a long day with a half dozen of good claret and a friend who didn't drink much. He opened the envelope, beamed at both teams, and began.

The compiler of questions for the league customarily put a few easy ones to start.

'First question, Grolden Brawl,' said our man. 'Where is a conning tower to be found on a submarine?'

Slightly puzzled, the Ball captain illustrated his point with a packet of Marlboro and a lighter, saying it was kind of half way along.

'No,' declared our man. 'And so over to MY team.'

His team were equally nonplussed. Yes, it is, we said, where they said it was.

'No,' declaimed the inquisitor, triumphantly. 'It's on a submarine.'

While the teams worked out that question and answer were liable to be read as one, the non-drinking friend offered to reduce the MC's workload by keeping the score. Quietly, he also began underlining the questions in red and the answers in blue. The MC continued.

'New Inn. Who in history are associated with the Pitcairn Islands?'

'Fletcher Christian. Captain Bligh. Mutiny on the Bounty,' said the New Inn captain, it always being good policy to give more than one answer in case of a too-literal judge.

'Quite correct,' said the MC. 'The Bountiny Mountaineers. Brolden Grawl, our esteemed visitors for tonight. What is the colour of the Predolican dollar?'

Not quite in tune yet with the novel experience they were having, the Golden Ball team took the question at face value and assumed that Predolica was a fictional country from a famous book they'd never read, and so had to admit ignorance. The New Inn team, more on the ball as it were, had deduced that what was required was the predominant colour of the American dollar, and so, correctly, said green.

Colour found its way into the next question too, when the Golden Ball were able to perceive that the red doll in Randy Andy was in fact the rag doll in Andy Pandy, and so had the point with Looby Loo.

And so the quiz took on a fourth dimension, with the teams having to know the answer as usual but first having to make divinations among the surreal verbal tangle that was the question. At the last, the MC did it for them.

'New Inn. In which soap opera is there a character who is a night-club singer? Don't know? Very well, over to our very good friends here this evening, our very good friends from The Grolden Brawl. Do you know? Hm? Do you know who is the soap club niner?'

CHAPTER EIGHT

The Pubs in Town

Harleston, in Norfolk, is not an overwhelmingly astonishing place. It's quite average, really, or typical, which is why it is interesting from the pub point of view. Like many small market towns, it once had a brewery and a goodly number of alehouses. Being on the London road to Great Yarmouth and, in the days of bad, bad roads, about a day's journey by carriage from that noteworthy seaport, it also had coaching inns, including a couple of very old ones. The exact age of some of the other pubs is difficult to tell, as most were owned by the Harleston Brewery before 1828 and individual licensees are not listed.

In that year, the brewery sold its estate, of 47 public houses in Norfolk and Suffolk, at an average price of around £700 including, in Harleston, The Swan for £1,400 and The Three Horseshoes for £325. Some of the properties went to Diss Brewery, called the Upper Brewery, later to be taken over by Lacon's of Great Yarmouth, which also fell later, to Whitbread. Some went to Tollemache, some to Cobbold, and some to individuals and small breweries but mostly and eventually ending up with Lacon's, or Steward and Patteson of Norwich, or Bullard's also of Norwich.

Population in the town was about 2,000 in 1883. In 1664 there were 80 households wealthy enough to pay the hearth tax, which is to say they were not paupers and had a house to live in. Modern Harleston has 1,850 households and a population of something over 4,000 so that, to be average, or typical, it should have four pubs.

The Swan, on the corner of the main street and Swan Lane, with its archway for coaches and its Georgian facade clearly added to an older building, proclaims itself to be what it is, an ancient purpose-built inn. The man who built it also opened it as the licensee in 1551, making this the most venerable pub now standing in the town, and he was Robert Cook, one of the many participants in Kett's Rebellion in 1549.

This was a rising against corrupt and incompetent government during the reign of the boy king Edward VI, especially against the unrestrained enclosure of common land by the upper classes – including, at one point,

The Swan Inn.

Robert Kett himself. A force of thousands, led by Kett, took Norwich, at that time the second city of the realm, and fought off an army but eventually, after many deaths, the rebellion was put down and all pardoned, including Cook but excepting some of the ringleaders. The brothers Kett, Robert and William, were hanged over the side of, respectively, Norwich Castle and Wymondham Abbey, their slow deaths being a warning to those of a rebellious nature.

Cook's new inn, called The White Swan, flourished, passed into the hands of the Harleston Brewery sometime after 1745, and became independent again in 1828, by which time it had long been established as an important stop on regular coach services. In the motor age, Trust Houses held it for 30 years, selling it in 1959 and it's been a free house ever since.

The other very old house in Harleston is not The Magpie, on the same London road and claiming 1584 as a founding date (see below), but The Cardinal's Hat, first licensee being a man of Yarmouth, Christopher Muriel, in 1591. Just under a century later, the owner of the Harleston Brewery bought it. We don't know what it was called then, but by the time it was sold to the Diss Brewery for £900 in 1828, it was The Colonel's Cap, thence to go through the Lacon's/Whitbread sequence like The Swan.

By the 1930s The Colonel had given his Cap to The Cardinal, why we don't know, but if it had stayed with the army it would have been the only pub in the UK thus named. As it is, there are four Cardinal's Hats.

The other coaching inn was The Magpie, later on the scene, being built around 1710 but with plenty of travellers' business to sustain it as well as The Swan and The Cap. The earlier date of 1584 claimed on the wall cannot refer to an inn nor other kind of licensed premises but may be connected with a dwelling on the site. Certainly a couple of very old cottages used to be in the yard, built way before 1710.

It was The Pye Inn in 1830; about 100 years later, the landlord, one Arthur Henry Bush, in lieu of cash for a bill, accepted an early work from local boy Alfred Munnings. Paintings by Munnings now fetch millions of dollars but, not long before World War Two began, the cost of bed, breakfast and dinner in The Magpie, at less than £1 a night, had to be afforded somehow.

This is the house that used to be The Hope and Anchor. The pitch of the roof defines it as originally thatched.

The wrought ironwork from which hung the sign of The Two Brewers is still there, but it's not been a pub for 50 years.

Then, and until 1977 when Lacon's sold it, The Magpie was the typical English market-place inn, with stuffed pike and photos of the otter hounds in the delightfully seedy saloon bar, and farmers in boots in the public bar on market day. The buyer in 1977 ripped the place apart. Now the old inn yard is a small housing estate and the hotel is much smarter.

Saying for sure which of the rest of the pubs is the oldest, is an impossible task. One strong contender for premises, if not licence, is The Hope and Anchor, closed by Steward and Patteson in the 1960s; first licensed in 1846 but in a house in a very old part of town, right by the market place – although not the old market place. Houses there are from 1450 to 1500; the Hope house would be a little later but not very much.

One you can still clearly see, a magnificent three-storey Georgian house in Broad Street, with parts going back further to the Sixteenth Century and additions in Victorian times, was The Two Brewers, owned by Harleston Brewery before 1828. It was still a Lacon's house as the 1960s began but it closed very soon after.

Possibly the oldest of the rest will be The Cherry Tree, another Harleston Brewery pub sold in 1828 but dating from at least a century before. The Aldous family had it until selling to the Adnams family in the early 1900s, who were relative newcomers to the industry, having bought the Sole Bay brewery in Southwold in 1872. The Cherry Tree represented an awfully big adventure, being their first, and for many years only, tied house outside Suffolk.

Crown House still has that signature that says 'I used to be a pub'.

The house on the right having a dish fitted has been identified elsewhere as The Three Horseshoes but it's rather more than 106 yards from The Cherry Tree. The pink cottage is a much older building but 106 yards marks a hole in the row where Kitchen Sense now stands.

The Crown on Mendham Lane, now a private house, was also part of the Harleston Brewery sale in 1828 but had not been built long before that. It opened and closed regularly in the late 1970s and 1980s but finally surrendered in 1996. It was just a good, little old boozer on the edge of town, now surrounded by housing estates that might have kept it afloat if they'd been there earlier. Some landlords have had interesting names such as Jabez Balls, Stebbings Leeder and Adolphus Stansbury, but its fate was sealed once it fell via Bullard's to Watney's.

The Three Horseshoes was 106 yards towards town from The Cherry Tree, sold to Cobbold in 1828 and on to Colchester Brewery, and closed by the magistrates in 1909.

The Royal Oak in Union Street fared worse, closing as a Cobbold house around 1900. The last of the Harleston Brewery sales was The Green Dragon, on the corner of the market place, to the Geldeston Brewery which was absorbed by Bullards. The magistrates completed their early Twentieth Century programme of closures with this pub, which was the subject of a compensation claim in 1910.

Oh no! Planners, in a town centre composed almost entirely of Tudor to Georgian buildings, how could you allow this ghastly boarded up modern excrescence? It stands where The Green Dragon last dispensed a pint of Bullard's in 1908.

The Duke William, like The Crown, couldn't be anything other than a dead pub.

The Railway Tavern. You can see where the barrels used to be rolled into the cellar.

It is difficult to explain why two of the 20 or so Duke Williams recently in business in the UK should be so close together, as the one in Redenhall Road, Harleston, and the one in neighbouring village Metfield, especially when the Duke in question, aka William the Conqueror, never visited the area as far as we know and died quite a while before either pub opened. It is equally difficult to see how any other William could have been meant. All the famous ones were not dukes, being kings, scholarly monks, a count (William the Silent) and a boy saint from Norwich.

Anyway, the Harleston Duke went the 1828 route via Diss Brewery, Lacon's and Whitbread until it closed, to be reopened as a free house in the 1980s. It struggled on but, at the time of writing, is closed and up for sale.

So, the only new, purpose-built pub in town since the beginning of the Nineteenth Century has to be The Railway Tavern, first licensed in 1861, not long after the railway itself arrived in Harleston, in 1855. Steward and Patteson bought it in 1903, so it became Watney's in 1967 and closed a few years after that. Briefly and bravely re-opened as a pub with a south-east Asian restaurant, it soon succumbed to Too Many Pubs syndrome around 1990.

How many pubs is too many?
In the Seventeenth Century on The Thoroughfare, there was Perosie's, later named The Half Moon and The Queen's Arms, briefly Tollemache's brewery then Lacon's, also a fishmonger's and a barber's at the same time as being a pub; licence refused in 1933. The Three Jolly Butchers was noted in 1839, and the old tollhouse became The White Horse and then Curls's shop also in the Nineteenth Century (now Sight and Sound). There was The Dog and Partridge on Broad Street, a Cobbold's house certainly until 1851, and The Horse and Groom likewise on that street around the same time. There was a beer house briefly on Chapel Street called The Plough, mid-Nineteenth Century. The Red Lion on Broad Street, a Steward and Patteson house, became the subscription library in 1884. The Grapes on The Thoroughfare became an off-licence in 1830, The Grapes Tap, owned by the Aldous family, and the Sir Robert Peel on Mendham Lane closed in 1896.

Up the road at Redenhall there was also The Eagle or Spread Eagle, of Colchester Brewery, closed in 1904, and The Yew Tree on Church Lane that became a private house in 1937. At its peak in the parish of Redenhall-with-Harleston, let us give a date of 1870, there were eighteen inns and beer houses operating, and another five had already been and gone.

We can say for sure that the population of men, women and children, in Redenhall village and Harleston, including that part of the town falling in the otherwise-Suffolk parish of Mendham, was a little over 2,000, including about 150 people, mostly men, listed as 'commercial', which is to say in trade, and about 60 as 'private' including a number of gentlewomen. A further quarter of the men worked on the land and there would be others, nominally heads of households, who worked for wages and so were not listed as tradesmen. How many were children we cannot tell.

It is hard to get from these figures more than, say, 700 potential pub customers and that's probably a generous estimate, or about 40 per pub. Still, the pubs survived, most of them, well into the modern age but, my, hasn't there been a sorting out of late.

Basically what's happened is that the three coaching inns have prospered, The Swan, The Cap and The Magpie, plus one of the bigger pubs, The Cherry Tree, owned by a vigorous local brewery and fortunate in its landlord during the time that Watney's were laying waste to Norfolk. The four pubs that have remained closed since 1960 were all owned then by local breweries but were taken over by national giants Whitbread and Watney, companies which would soon cease brewing altogether. Probably they would have closed anyway. So, we're left with four pubs in town, for a population of almost 4,000. Typical.

Famous Last Words

A song by George and Ira Gershwin was about romantic love between persons unknown but it could equally apply to our love of pubs. Television, cheap supermarket booze and all the other pressures may be making pub-love more and more difficult but, we say, our love is here to stay.

> It's very clear
> Our love is here to stay
> Not for a year, but ever and a day
> The radio
> And the telephone
> And the movies that we know
> May just be passing fancies
> and in time may go
> But oh my dear
> Our love is here to stay
> Together we're going a long long way
> In time the Rockies may crumble
> Gibraltar may tumble
> They're only made of clay
> But our love is here to stay